D1624289

| Wallace Library | DUE DATE (stamped in blue) |
	RETURN DATE (stamped in black)

AN EYE FOR WINNERS

AN EYE FOR WINNERS

How I Built One of America's Great Businesses— And So Can You

Lillian

LILLIAN VERNON

HarperBusiness
A Division of HarperCollinsPublishers

A hardcover edition of this book was published in 1996 by HarperBusiness, a division of HarperCollins Publishers.

AN EYE FOR WINNERS. Copyright © 1996 by Lillian Vernon. All rights reserved. Printed in the United States of America. No part of this book may be used or reproduced in any manner whatsoever without written permission except in the case of brief quotations embodied in critical articles and reviews. For information address HarperCollins Publishers, Inc., 10 East 53rd Street, New York, NY 10022.

HarperCollins books may be purchased for educational, business, or sales promotional use. For information please write: Special Markets Department, HarperCollins Publishers, Inc., 10 East 53rd Street, New York, NY 10022.

First paperback edition published 1997.

Designed by Nancy Singer

The Library of Congress has catalogued the hardcover edition as follows:

Vernon, Lillian, 1927–
    An eye for winners : how I built one of America's greatest direct-mail businesses / Lillian Vernon.
        p. cm.
    ISBN 0-88730-818-X
    1. Vernon, Lillian, 1927–   . 2. Women in business—United States—Biography. 3. Mail-order business—United States—History. I. Title.
HF5466.V367   1996
381'.142'092—dc20
[B]   96-9312

ISBN 0-88730-879-1 (pbk.)

97 98 99 00 01 ❖/RRD 10 9 8 7 6 5 4 3 2 1

To Fred, David, Paolo,
and to all of you
who mean so much to me.
My wish is that you
become the person you
most want to be.

CONTENTS

ACKNOWLEDGMENTS

I have loved writing this book. Throughout the many months I relived so many wonderful memories—some very sad, most of them joyous. I have lived an extraordinary life, and I'm happy to be able to share it with you. We can all make our own miracles!

I wish to thank my sons, Fred and David Hochberg, whom I love unconditionally, for their support and encouragement. In loving memory of my mother, father, and brother who are always in my heart.

Without my family, loyal customers, and all the people at Lillian Vernon, this book would not have been possible.

A special thank you to Donna Carpenter, to my dear friend and agent, Joni Evans, and to my editor at HarperCollins, Adrian Zackheim. They have made a difference and are the best.

ENTREPRENEURIAL QUIZ

Are You a Natural-Born Entrepreneur?

One of the greatest pleasures of my career is meeting people from all over the world who have a talent for turning dreams into reality. I'm not just talking about big business executives, either. Many are individuals who have an instinct for developing good ideas into successful business ventures.

Since my book was first published, I've received thousands of letters asking me what I think an entrepreneur must have to succeed. Of course, success is the result of many factors, but I have found that successful entrepreneurs share many common characteristics. This short quiz will help you decide if you have what it takes to start your own business. Choose one answer per question.

1. When you work late or on the weekends do you:
   a) feel you're entitled to a raise
   b) consider it part of the job
   c) feel you should be compensated with time off

2. Would you rather start your own business:
   a) with a new product and an undeveloped market
   b) by buying an existing company
   c) with a developed market for an existing product

3. As a successful entrepreneur would you:
   a) hire experts to run your business
   b) keep things small enough manage yourself
   c) stay in charge and on top of every detail

4. When obstacles keep you from making progress do you:
   a) persist until you get what you want
   b) drop the project and move on to something more productive
   c) delegate the task to someone with more time and knowledge

5. To succeed in business would you rather:
   a) beat the current competition at their own game
   b) find a different market niche and then fill it
   c) have a familiar brand or company name behind you

6. Which best describes your personality when it comes to making money:
   a) willing to take risks
   b) good at analyzing risk
   c) good at avoiding risk

7. To get something done right, do you:
   a) do it yourself
   b) work with others who share your goal
   c) delegate to skilled professionals

8. You have the afternoon all to yourself. Would you rather:
   a) get organized at home
   b) read a book at home
   c) go out shopping

9. You are alone in a foreign country. Would you prefer to:
   a) take an organized tour
   b) visit a special attraction with others who share your interests
   c) explore on your own

10. When it comes to managing your money, do you prefer:
    a) electronic/computerized banking
    b) having someone else manage your money
    c) personally handling the accounting and check writing

Scoring:

Use this table to add up your points. You get a set number of points for each question answered. Your final score will provide insight into your own entrepreneurial nature.

1) a-1	b-3	c-2
2) a-3	b-1	c-2
3) a-1	b-2	c-3
4) a-1	b-3	c-2
5) a-2	b-1	c-1
6) a-3	b-2	c-1
7) a-2	b-3	c-1
8) a-3	b-1	c-2
9) a-1	b-3	c-2
10) a-3	b-1	c-2

23-30 points: You have the spirit of an entrepreneur. Ideas probably come easily to you and you have good business instincts. Starting from scratch does not phase you. You forge ahead despite obstacles and gain confidence along the way. You are a dreamer who accepts risk as a part of life, but you don't commit to things blindly. People like you prefer to plan carefully, keep up with details, and stay in charge. Read my book for some perspective and inspiration.

14-22 points: You have a good head for business, but uncertainty can make you nervous. You're likely to be cautious by nature, but your passion for good ideas can drive you to succeed. While others may only talk about their dreams you are likely to be the "doer" in the crowd, able to finish what you start even if you have to ask others for help along the way. I would urge you to explore your entrepreneurial leaning. Just don't bite off more than you can chew at first and learn from your experiences. As with any business venture, don't pass off too much responsibility to others you deem as experts. Master all facets of your business as it grows.

0-13 points: You may lack the necessary mindset to start your own business. Are you sure you would enjoy being the entrepreneur who wears many hats and works nights, weekends, and on your own? Entrepreneurs have a "start-to-finish" vision that keeps complex ventures squarely on track. If juggling the many complex details of running a business might overwhelm you, a corporate setting may be your better choice.

1

ONE WOMAN'S HEART

A Born Entrepreneur

—

A Woman in Business

—

Repaying My Debts

—

Questions and Answers

—

Mail order is truly an American business. Like so many other great U.S. institutions, it was founded by Benjamin Franklin. In his very first catalog of scientific and academic books, which he published in 1744, Franklin included a reassuring guarantee of delivery: "Those persons who live remote, by sending their orders and money to said B. Franklin may depend on the same justice as if present." Knowing what we do about the man's integrity and business savvy, we can be certain he lived up to his promise. And given the way mail-order businesses have flourished in the decades since, we know "those persons who live remote" did indeed send in their orders and their money. In 1872, Aaron Montgomery Ward shipped his catalog to farmers through-out the Midwest. In 1886, Richard W. Sears followed suit. Sears, along with his partner, Alva Roebuck, created not only a catalog but American folk history as well. In 1912, L. L. Bean initiated his enduring catalog when he offered far-flung shoppers a hunting boot with a lifetime guarantee.

When I took my first tentative steps in mail order, years ago, I had no aspirations to folk history, fame, or fortune. I was a young homemaker, pregnant with my first child, trying to make ends meet. I was hardworking, I was hopeful, and, frankly, I was naïve. What was I thinking when I started all this back in 1951? Only this: perhaps I can earn enough money to pay some household bills and ease our family's financial concerns. You could say that I entered the business world through the back door. Yet my small enterprise, started with an investment of $2,000, has grown into a substantial organization that brings in revenues of more than $240 million annually—all of which goes to prove that sometimes a little naïveté can be a useful thing.

Direct marketing, simply put, is selling retail directly to a business. Mail-order businesses offer merchandise through newspaper and magazine ads, catalogs, radio, and, more recently, through television—especially cable TV. Many of us advertise on the Internet, and even produce our own CD-ROMs.

Mail-order revenues have grown to more than $62.6 billion. With the introduction of credit cards and the toll-free 800-numbers, the mail-order business received a major boost. Customers could get speedy delivery by calling in and charging their orders, without bothering to fill out forms, purchase money orders, or put up with delays. The first toll-free numbers—introduced in 1967—only made buying by phone more irresistible. By the early 1990s, more than half of the adult population of the United States did a portion of its shopping from catalogs, increasing mail-order revenues by 52 percent between 1984 and 1994.

Despite compelling evidence to the contrary, certain analysts have more than once predicted the imminent demise of mail order. First the telephone was going to kill it: people would dial stores directly to place their orders and toss catalogs out with yesterday's newspaper. Then it was the automobile: all the glorious highways we built after the World War II would induce people to leave their homes and drive to department stores and shopping malls. I guess the crystal balls didn't pick up on the impact of traffic jams, gas shortages, parking fines, and snowstorms. I guess the crystal balls didn't pick up on a lot. In fact, they were, I'm glad to report, dead wrong.

There are many reasons for the big jump in catalog shopping—some perfectly obvious, some hard to define. The increasing numbers of women who've entered the workforce had a major impact: fewer people now have time to go to stores. Why waste precious Saturday afternoons or desperately needed lunch breaks trying to accomplish what can be done right from your desk? Why deal with indifferent clerks or long lines at the register? With the printing and production quality of catalogs higher than ever, there's little doubt about the exact look and the quality of products you can buy from the comfort and safety of your home.

Mail order today is a big and growing business. It has simplified people's lives, expanded their purchasing options, and handed them more free time. I'm glad to have opened that back door all those years ago and entered into this business. I'm honored to have played a part in it and, on my own terms, to have remained a part of it today.

A Born Entrepreneur

Recently, my foundation had the enormous privilege of endowing a chair of entrepreneurship at New York University—the Lillian Vernon Professorship. To expose students to different points of view, the university will name a new professor to the chair every three years. I couldn't be more pleased. After attending New York City public schools, I completed my own formal education at NYU. By completed, I mean I studied for two years and then left to get married. But what I learned in those years has stayed with me. Professor Thomas Cochrane, a kind of early mentor, taught me the merits of independent thought and rigorous mental self-discipline. I learned the importance of clear-headed analysis and came to understand how an honest appraisal of my personality and business could prove invaluable. I've always felt indebted to NYU, and this $1.5 million endowment is my way of giving back. I hope that others will learn as much there as I did. Perhaps more, after the endorsement of the Lillian Vernon Professorship.

In my student days, *entrepreneur* was a word you didn't come across outside French class. There was no formal guidance in this area, no instruction. Looking back, I realize I am an entrepreneur by nature. My greatest business skills were gained the hard way—on my own. I learned by doing, by making choices, and by making mistakes. At first, many attributed my early success to luck. I started with one small ad in a magazine for teenage girls. The ad—promoting monogrammed bags and belts—cost $495. In three months we sold $32,000 of goods. Who wouldn't feel lucky? I knew nothing about strategic planning and financial projections. I was running on my most valuable ally—my golden gut, trying to stay solvent and sane. Sometimes I look back and wonder how I managed to remain either.

A Woman in Business

When I began my business, mail order was a man's domain. Women were expected to be wives and mothers. Ambitious, capable women were regarded warily. Luckily, I never gave too much credence to conventional wisdom or common prejudices. My husband and I needed a little more money. I had an idea about how to make some.

In the course of my business dealings, nobody ever took advantage of me simply because I was a woman. Men did, however, feel entitled to a discouraging amount of condescension and patronizing behavior. When my company became a big supplier to Revlon in 1963, I was told that Charles Revson was surprised to hear that a woman headed the Lillian Vernon Corporation. Why did he think the name wasn't a woman's? When I shopped for merchandise at trade fairs, suppliers would frequently ask, "Are you buying for a gift shop?" or "Do you run a little business in your basement, dear?" My feelings of annoyance and outrage were tempered by delight at knowing that my "little business" was outgrossing them all. Fortunately, attitudes have changed. Women in business still face hurdles, but on the whole, we're treated with the respect we've earned. It pleases me that my company's success has contributed to this shift in attitudes, opened some minds and more than a few doors.

WORKING AT HOME

When I started my business in 1951, I did it as a matter of necessity. We needed money, and I, four months pregnant, had to stay at home. I don't know how many people worked from home in those days, but there were fewer then than there are today. According to the latest figures, over forty million Americans work at home, and that number is growing by about 12 percent each year.

There are many reasons for this development. Downsizing and layoffs at large companies have compelled men and women to find new ways to earn their living. Women who are tied to their homes, as I was, are trying to make more money to stretch the shrinking family budget. The desire for independence is another powerful motivator. And no one misses the stress of commuting. For women who do not enjoy housework, there is yet another advantage; housework is no longer their prime occupation.

Many successful mail-order businesses can trace their roots back to spare bedrooms and unused garages, but before you commit yourself to that course, you should force yourself to answer some pointed questions. If you have not worked before, you may be better prepared than people who have acquired an office mentality. It's quite common for someone accustomed to working with others to feel isolated and at loose ends when setting up shop at home.

You may find that you have to draw on all the self-discipline you can muster, and you will certainly have to develop some hard-and-fast working rules. Can you be tough enough to turn away drop-in friends or cut short personal telephone calls? You'll have to make it clear to friends that you can't chat during working hours. At the same time, though, you don't want to cut yourself off from all daily contact with the outside world. Join a club or a group, and make a point of meeting people for specific business events. If you do that, you won't miss the gregariousness of office life.

It helps if you can set aside a specific room or part of the house for your work. Our first apartment was so small that I worked in the kitchen. In any case, you should make sure you really like working at home. Some people do not. If spending both waking and sleeping hours at home does not appeal to you, it may—if you can afford it—be worth the expense to rent space elsewhere.

When I first began my mail-order business, I was prepared to work—and often did—from early in the morning until late at night, squeezing my household and family chores in between. As soon as I could afford it, I hired a cleaning person.

It didn't take me long to discover that it helps to set certain specific goals for each day and to maintain a schedule. Don't let your concentration slip. Reorganize your home priorities so that they dovetail with the hours you need to spend working and working very hard.

If you plan to work at home, your drive and commitment to your business is absolutely critical. I loved my business, and I never resented the time and energy it demanded. Always remember, you are now your own boss, working on your own turf. This will be your source of strength.

Be sure to check with your accountant to see what percentage of your home expenses are tax deductible and what you are legally entitled to.

Repaying My Debts

You might think that today I'd be ready to sit back and relax. When I started, I would have thought so. Instead, I'm just as busy as I was when my sons were growing up and my business was expanding. In addition to my duties as CEO and chairman of the Lillian Vernon Corporation, I'm involved in a variety of charitable activities. I want to repay what I consider my debt to a country that has rewarded me so generously. I serve on the boards of many nonprofit organizations. Because I love the arts, I'm on the board of New York's Lincoln Center, the New York Film Festival, and the Virginia Opera. I also work with the American Friends of the Israel Philharmonic, the Kennedy Center, and the National Actors Theater.

Outside of the arts, I am on the executive committee of City Meals On Wheels and serve on the Board of Overseers of New York University's College of Arts & Science.

Even though fourteen senior managers help me run the Lillian Vernon Corporation, and my two sons, Fred and David Hochberg, are independent adults with lives of their own, I still seem to be short of time. My commitments outside the company last year demanded as much schedule juggling as I practiced when I was running the company alone and raising my children. The evening I get to spend at home, quietly reading, heading off to bed early, is a rare event.

My work has put me in a certain limelight. I'm no celebrity, but, according to a National Opinion Research Poll, over forty-seven million Americans recognize my name, and one in four American households receives the Lillian Vernon catalog. In restaurants and airports, people approach me with a congratulatory word or an expression of respect for what I've done. That's thrilling and unbelievably gratifying. People have even asked me to autograph copies of my catalog, something I take delight in, especially because so much of my business has been based on personalized merchandise. I'm proud of what I've accomplished, and I'm glad to say it. If my words give encouragement to those contemplating their own ventures, so much the better.

Questions and Answers

To what, many people have asked, do I owe my success? How did I find the merchandise, and how did I deal with finances, customers, employees, and the myriad responsibilities of the mail-order business? How did I meet such demands and manage to raise a family at the same time while engaging in an active social life of travel, parties, and commitment to the private sector?

That's the story, with all the many ups and downs, I'm going to tell you. I've often described the mail-order business as the agony and the ecstasy. Agony when you've picked your merchandise, sent out the catalog, and are waiting for customers to respond. Agony when such uncontrollable forces as the weather derail your careful schedule. Agony when a product bombs. But ecstasy when customers love the merchandise you've carefully selected. Ecstasy when you hear from satisfied buyers. Ecstasy when sales exceed even your wildest expectations.

For over four decades, the Lillian Vernon Corporation has been my passion, my companion, and—when things were rough—my solace. It's the thread that runs through all the years of my adult life, through my two marriages, first to Samuel Hochberg, the father of my sons, and then to Robert Katz, through the births and raising of my two sons, Fred and David. In many ways, it's been the most important part of my life. But it is only part. Difficult as much of it has been, I see my life, all in all, as a glorious adventure. The difficult times, as well as the good, have brought me to where I am right now. I ask you to join me as I look back and relive that adventure.

2

MENACED BY A SHADOW

The year was 1932, the day December 12. I was a little girl, and this was a big party. Relatives from across Germany sat at a horseshoe-shaped dining table bedecked with fine crystal, gleaming silver, elegant china, and sumptuous food. It was the tenth wedding anniversary of my parents, Herman and Erna.

The celebration was well-earned. My father, Herman Menasche, with my mother's help, had grown prosperous in the lingerie trade. We lived in an imposing brick villa on a tree-lined street in Leipzig, Germany. There was a small pond on our extensive grounds, and in winter, when the surface was magically transformed into a layer of cold glistening ice, we held skating parties for relatives and friends. We were a well-off family, respected and happy. In the accepted upper-class European fashion of the time, my mother, Erna, had turned the care of her children—my older brother, Fred, and me—over to nannies when we were babies and to a governess when we got older. We were taught to bow or curtsy when we shook hands with adults. We rarely argued with our parents, and at an event such as that party, we knew we were expected to remain deferentially quiet unless asked a question. Those formalities didn't diminish my pleasure one bit.

My mother was a renowned beauty, a five-foot-three-inch brunette who dressed with Viennese flair. My father was exceptionally intelligent and possessed a remarkable natural ability to solve problems. He was tall, olive-complected, and wore his shiny black hair slicked back in dashing movie-star fashion. He, too, dressed with elegance and rarely appeared in public without a starched white handkerchief in the breast pocket of his suit. There were times when he shouted at us, but more with concern than anger; he cared fiercely about his children, always wanting us to do our best. My mother was always more judgmental. She could be harsh in her criticism, and often her words stung. She kept her distance from her children—perhaps a greater distance from me than from my brother. Over the years, I struggled to understand her and gain her approval, but I never grew as close to her as I did to my father.

In his later years, my father faced many adversities in business. I remember seeing him weep openly only once, when his first venture in the United States, a lingerie manufacturing business, failed. He was, at heart, an optimistic man—a fighter who refused to give in when circumstances conspired against him. I shall always be grateful to him because I believe that his optimism and determination are part of his legacy to me. They are traits that have buoyed my spirits and renewed my vigor whenever life has turned rough.

The Swastika

That December evening of my parents' anniversary—so warm with love and happiness—is one of my favorite memories. Ironically, it also marked the end of our privileged life and, in a real sense, my childhood.

On January 30, 1933—a mere six weeks later—Adolf Hitler became chancellor of Germany. The atmosphere in Leipzig and throughout Germany darkened. Fear crept into our lives. Taunts of "Jüde, Jüde, Jüde" assaulted my brother, Fred, and me as we walked to school. Everywhere we went, we heard hysterical shouts of "Heil Hitler." It was impossible to turn on the radio without hearing of some fresh attack that had been launched against Jewish citizens. A new flag—red, white, and black with a swastika emblazoned on it—hung from government buildings and on many private houses. I know I no longer need to fear that symbol of Nazism, but even today, when I see a swastika on television or in a movie,

I experience an echo of the fear and bewildered panic that plagued me during those years.

One day, as I listened to Fred practice the piano in the music room, I heard a loud banging that reverberated throughout the house. The Nazis were at the door. Brutal-looking thugs wearing swastikas ordered us to leave our house at once. They turned the home we loved and were so proud of, the home my father had struggled for years to afford, into Nazi headquarters.

We moved into a nearby second-floor apartment. From a window in the back we could see our old house, and in anger and despair we watched the Nazi usurpers swagger in and out of our front door. Ice sealed over the pond's surface that winter, but there were no parties, no laughing skaters, no soaring bonfires. When I tried to play in the garden attached to our apartment house, I was rebuffed by the other children because I was Jewish.

Many in our circle denied the danger Hitler posed to German Jews. Affluent and educated, they considered themselves as much a part of German society, and certainly as patriotic, as Hitler and his brown-shirted troops. Many had fought bravely, many had been wounded, and some had died fighting for Germany in the trenches of World War I. Surely the persecution of Jews was a passing phenomenon. How could it be otherwise? Soon it would stop.

Exactly the opposite happened. Two years after we were forced out of our house, a gang of Nazi youths, screaming "Jüde," chased Fred home and threw him down the stairs of our apartment house. I can still see the blood streaming down his left cheek and the look of confused horror in his eyes.

Escape

The attack on my brother, Fred, confirmed my father's decision to emigrate. The time had come to leave Leipzig and what had once been our beloved country. My father made plans to move to Amsterdam. The thriving Dutch city had, for many centuries, welcomed Jewish exiles, and he assumed it would be a safe refuge for us, too. He saw the move as inevitable, but that made it no less difficult. He was forced to leave all his business assets behind—everything he had pinned his hopes on. In Amsterdam, he would have to start all over again. It was a wrenching farewell. He knew that our family faced a precarious future.

Upheaval was nothing new to Central Europeans, many of whom had been forced to live with uncertainty since the outbreak of World War I in 1914. My mother told us what happened to her family, diamond merchants in Antwerp, Belgium, when the Germans attacked in August of that year. Austria was Germany's ally, and her family, originally Austrian citizens, was ordered to leave home with only a few hours' notice. They were allowed to take with them only what they could carry—the family silver and jewelry. They moved first to live with relatives in Berlin, later Cracow, and they later returned to Berlin, where my parents met and married. The rest of my mother's family had moved back to Antwerp, where they still live.

In 1933, I was a young girl—still not fully aware of the evil stalking us across Europe. We were going to Holland: the land of Hans Brinker, chocolates, cheeses, tulips, windmills, and wooden shoes. For a child, it wasn't an escape or an exile, but an exciting adventure.

At first, school in Amsterdam was hard. We didn't know the language. The children teased Fred and me, calling us *Moffe,* slang for "Germans," but their taunts carried none of the malevolence we had endured in Leipzig. All the same, I was lonely. Now, as a businesswoman, I understand that there are advantages to being an outsider peering in. Outsiders see with a special clarity. As we strolled the cobbled streets, I watched and took note of the foreign life around me. I was especially interested in people's shopping habits. Why was this store crowded with customers and that one empty? What were people looking for when they gazed into shop windows? What made them enter this shop and walk past that one? I am convinced that my observations at that early age guided me toward my later decision to go into business. That solitary little girl, wandering along the romantic canals of Amsterdam, acquired, albeit unconsciously, a skill she could later put to good account.

Skill alone is not enough, though: it leads nowhere without training and hard work. In my family, nothing was more valued than achievement, learning how to do something well. None of us stopped until we had done our best. The early pressure to achieve, which has served me well, has also made it hard for me to relax. In my early adulthood, guilt nagged me whenever I was not working, and, to this day, I find myself fighting a vague uneasiness in those rare idle moments.

Amsterdam, a city of exile, quickly became home. My father started a small factory where he produced simple housecoats, dowdy but practical. He made enough to support us, albeit in a style quite different from the one we'd been used to in Leipzig: our Dutch apartment was a third-floor walk-up that offered basic comforts with few frills. My mother, who'd always hated the drudgery of cooking and housework, asked one of our German maids to accompany us to Holland. I have a vivid memory of Hilda, a plump, rosy-cheeked woman who worked diligently but silently. Her cheerful appearance belied her mean-spiritedness and a streak of cruelty that would soon cause us trouble.

My mother noticed that Hilda had started to linger at the door of our living room whenever we had guests. Was it our paranoia, or was she paying especially close attention whenever the talk turned to Hitler? We were about to find out. She came into our living room one day, planted her feet firmly, and announced that she'd noted our guests had nothing good to say about "Our Führer." She turned to my mother and said, "I'm reporting you to the German consulate."

My mother paled, but she gathered her strength and stood. Although small in stature, at that moment she seemed to tower above Hilda. "You listen to me," she said, her voice steady and proud. "I am no longer a German citizen. We were forced to leave our country, our home, everything we worked for and loved, all to save our lives. We're free people living in Holland, and we won't be intimidated by you. You yourself told me your fiancé was critical of Hitler. If you denounce us, I'll report him."

An hour later, Hilda was gone. She may have been a spy for the Nazis. We never saw her again. The last tie with my German childhood was broken.

Search for Safety

My father, watching events in Germany, realized that it was necessary, once again, to move on. He decided to investigate Palestine—Israel, as we call it today. And so, at the age of five, I was off on a six-week sea voyage full of new sights and adventures, and more excitement.

Some events in my life have left indelible impressions— but not always for the most obvious reasons. After we'd been at sea for a couple of weeks, we ran into unusually bad weather. The crew lashed down everything movable and all but closed the kitchens; the passengers retreated to their cabins. I have vague memories of the way the ship's hull shuddered as we plowed into the mountainous waves, of the creaking and groaning, as if the boat itself were crying out for help. But what I remember most vividly is this: hours into the storm, my father and Fred went off to look in on one of our shipmates. My mother and I were alone in the narrow confines of our cabin when a wave seemed to rip through the hull. Mother rushed to me and threw her arms around me. "We're going down," she said, "but this way, we'll at least go down together." She was not a woman given to easy displays of affection. With her arms around me, I felt protected from the howling winds, the cold green water, whatever nature had in store for us. In that moment, I felt sure of her love. When the storm had abated and life on board returned to normal, my mother retreated to her usual distance and I was left once again with my doubts about her true feelings.

Immediately after that drama, I was stricken with pneumonia and forced to spend a large part of the voyage isolated in my cabin. When I was finally allowed on deck again, the other passengers gave a big cheer that I can still hear. People had noticed my absence! As the daughter of an unaffectionate mother, it was the kind of affirmation I desperately longed for.

Palestine then was quite different from Israel today. Its barren landscape seemed hostile to a child used to the green grass and trees of northern Europe. Not until the founding of Israel, in 1948, did its people begin to irrigate extensively. We went to visit my father's brother, Uncle Sigmund, who lived in Tel Aviv in a small walk-up apartment with his wife, Sophia, and three daughters, my cousins Lucy, Ruth, and Judith. He never succeeded in business in Palestine, and in the end, his failure may have influenced my father. Doubting he could make a living there, my father decided not to settle. That country's future was as uncertain as our own. We headed back to Amsterdam. We traveled to Leipzig to see my grandmother, and I was taken to a Nazi parade and saluted Hitler with the rest of the crowd.

Upon our return, my father was devastated to discover that his partner had embezzled the capital from his housecoat business. I learned later that, in addition to money, his partner had stolen something less tangible and perhaps more important: he robbed my father of his trust in people. Money can be replaced; trust, not so easily. The upshot of that disaster was that for the second time my father had to begin anew. He remained in the manufacture of housecoats because that's where his expertise lay. Slowly, methodically, he rebuilt the business, reinforcing an example that would last me through all my own setbacks and renewals.

We lived in Holland for two more years. As I was beginning to feel truly at home and comfortable, my parents started to talk about yet another move. By 1937, it was clear that Germany was on the move, poised for conquest. They could easily see what some of England's and France's leaders refused to see. We would have to leave again: this time we'd sail across the ocean to the United States.

Arrival

My parents left for New York City, leaving Fred and me in the care of our maternal grandmother, Fanny Feiner. She and her three other children, Pala Zweibel, Helene Russhandler, and Jacques Feiner, lived not far away, in Antwerp. My father knew that time was against him, and he had to establish himself in the United States as quickly as possible. He spoke no English and had few connections. Yet it took him only three months to get a start in the housecoat and negligee business and to rent an apartment. He must have worked furiously. When it was time for Fred and me to join our parents, my mother came to Amsterdam to escort us. Upon her return, she discovered that our American visas—our lifeline to the future—were due to expire. Refugees from Germany were begging for visas, and she was frightened that we might not be able to get ours renewed. Luck was on our side. A sympathetic consulate official gave her the extension and let her know—without quite saying it—that peril was at our gate.

Though I was still a child, I could sense that something grim was threatening our world. My parents were host to many German Jews forced out of their homeland. Every conversation focused obsessively on upheaval and uncertainty. How would they make their livings? Where could they escape to now? All of Europe was unsafe. If they didn't know English, they would have to learn it. The future offered them nothing but the fearful unknown. My parents and their friends always seemed to be on the brink of disaster. I think the atmosphere of imminent doom in which we lived during my formative years led to a lifelong sense of panic and anxiety. Will I be safe tomorrow? Will I survive? Overcoming those fears has been a lifelong battle, and many days—even now—I wonder if finally it will ever be won.

I know the story of Anne Frank. I can visualize where she lived, it was so near our own apartment in Amsterdam. I often think, but for the grace of God, there go my family. Some of our relatives did not get out of Europe, but they were luckier than the Franks. Their hiding places were never discovered, and they survived the German occupation in Antwerp, Belgium. One cousin spent the war years in a convent—no doubt going to mass every day. Her name is Ruth, but the nuns changed it to a French name—Simone. My grandmother, an uncle, an aunt, his wife, her husband, and three children were hidden by Belgian families in the country. My Aunt Regine risked her life every day to bring them food. Just after the war, my Aunt Regine had a stillborn baby because of the appalling diet and stress she had endured during those years. My grandmother and my other relatives were extraordinarily resilient and I admired their courage and determination.

Some of my father's family escaped by moving to Palestine. One brother, Josef, moved to Manchester, England, where he was joined by my grandmother, who'd been living in Italy. My uncle Jacob, with his wife, Sally, arrived in the United States at the last possible moment before the outbreak of war in 1939. Every member of the family escaped death by the Nazis except, finally, my brother, Sigfried (affectionately called Fred or Freddy).

The Statue of Liberty

On October 17, 1937, my mother, Fred, and I steamed into New York harbor and gazed, enthralled, at the Statue of

Liberty. The ship anchored off shore, where immigration officials came on board. Imagine our reaction when we recognized my father among them! I have never figured out how he did it. . . . Perhaps that quality of a "doer."

Our ship, the *Staatendam*, docked in Hoboken, and we boarded the subway for New York City. Fred and I could hardly contain our excitement as we perched on the subway's shiny, hard, yellow woven-straw seats. The first time I set foot on the glamorous island of Manhattan, I was emerging from the subway.

Initially, we stayed with a relative who lived on the Upper West Side; then, for a brief time, we lived in a hotel. Before long, however, we moved into our own place.

Our first home was an old-fashioned six-room apartment on Ninety-seventh Street on Manhattan's Upper West Side—high-ceilinged, comfortable, and spacious. The rent was $75 a month. My parents furnished it with the few antiques they had been able to transport and whatever affordable extras they could find. The pleasant neighborhood of wide avenues and quiet side streets was nestled between the Hudson River and Central Park. Broadway was lined with shops of every imaginable description, and West End Avenue, with its stately apartment houses, reminded us of nineteenth-century Vienna. The side streets were home to some of New York City's finest brownstones. There were so many German, and later Austrian, refugees who settled in that part of the city that it was not unusual to get on a bus and hear almost nothing but German.

An Outsider Looking In

Two days after our arrival in New York, I was sitting at a worn wooden school desk in Manhattan's Public School 93, a red brick building that took up half the block, on Ninety-third Street between Broadway and Amsterdam Avenue. In those days, classes were segregated: boys in one, girls in another. Our teachers were tough-minded women, many of them Irish, who knew how to teach.

By chance, my first day of classes was "treat day." Other students had brought cookies and candy to swap at the mid-morning snack, but I had nothing. Sitting in the back of the room, I felt completely isolated. And I knew no English, so I couldn't understand a word anyone said.

Then, a girl, Shirley Newman—my first American friend—made her way toward my desk and shyly put down a piece of candy. One by one, the other girls followed until my desk was covered with treats. I nearly wept with grati-tude—my first experience of American generosity. I was glad that I did at least know how to say "Thank you."

Before we left Amsterdam, we had celebrated my broth-er's bar mitzvah. Uncle Isidore Reichwald, who had emi-grated to England in 1935, understood that Fred would be the center of attention so he had brought a little present for me—a nesting toy, a large egg containing a smaller egg, and so on down to the tiniest, which contained a little chick. It was the perfect present, and I loved it.

Although American hospitality made life much easier for me, there were times when Fred and I were lonely. We were foreigners. We didn't know the language. At first we spoke Dutch with each other—the switch to English was gradual. We didn't know the customs of the country. We had no estab-lished friends—no other children with whom we had shared experiences. As in Amsterdam, I felt like an outsider. I belonged to one of those clubs that young girls love to form. There were four of us in it, all from the same neighborhood. When Christmas came, one of the girls gave each of us a scrapbook, but, before she handed them over, she measured them carefully. One was smaller than the other two, and that's the one she gave to me. Silly memories sometimes stay the longest.

To keep up our spirits, Fred and I drew on our family tra-dition of tenacity and enterprise. Together, we worked hard to master English and to understand the bewildering world around us. We were closer than we had ever been, and I treasure the memory of those times we spent trying out our new language and comparing notes on American customs. I especially remember my first pair of penny loafers. It was said, "As long as you wear penny loafers, you will never be broke." Fred, who was four years older, inherited our father's dark looks. He was slim and nearly six feet tall. He liked to play chess with his friends, but sometimes he would retire to his own little back room to bounce a ball against the wall for hours on end. He never lost all traces of his accent, but I was young enough, with practice, to get rid of mine. Our parents spoke German to each other, but English with us. I dearly loved my brother, and although my parents focused on him as the only son in a European family, I never felt a twinge of jealousy. He was my support and friend during those early years.

My father's lingerie manufacturing business, which he named Mercury Products, wasn't going well. He had two uncles in New York who were successful businessmen, but he never asked them for help. He was too proud and independent, and he was determined to make it on his own.

The atmosphere at home was often tense. My parents were competitive, and the two of them had always argued. When life got really tough for them, they fought even more. I never saw any overt gestures of affection between them, but I have this example of their love. Once, when my mother had a little cyst, she went to the doctor to have it removed. To her great relief, she was told it was benign. She informed me later that my father had "kissed me in the street, he was so happy." Nonetheless, disagreements were frequent and often ended with one or the other stalking out of the house.

Into the Kitchen

Mother spent her first two months in New York setting up house. Then she went to work with my father. She acted as

BOOTSTRAPPING

Bootstrapping is the word we use these days to describe starting a business with very little money. To keep going, bootstrappers rely completely on their wits to generate a sustaining cash flow. You begin your enterprise with no financial cushion. You have to hold to a tight budget, and you have to use every technique you can to generate cash simply to stay alive. It's not at all rare for a beginning entrepreneur to make deliveries personally, use a wooden packing case as a desk, or impress potential customers or clients by faking a secretarial voice on the telephone. Any stratagem is valid if it nurtures your cash situation and your business.

A bootstrapper gears every outlay toward maximizing cash flow and cuts costs and corners any way possible. Beginners must never forget that the key to business success is money.

the supervisor and worked alongside the staff. "Your father needs me in the business," she said to me one evening. "Starting tomorrow, your job will be to shop and make dinner for the family."

After school, I'd walk to the butcher's and the vegetable store (there were no supermarkets then), and wait in line with the grown-ups, then hurry home to prepare dinner. Since the Upper West Side was a favorite nesting place for German-Jewish refugees, the storekeepers, many of them Jewish immigrants themselves, catered to European tastes. I learned to cook by trial and error, and I soon had no problems preparing meals. We ate good meals every day. I spent hours in that old-fashioned, dark kitchen. It had a porcelain sink, an inadequate oven, a refrigerator that had to be defrosted once a week, and a small window that overlooked an interior courtyard. I've always relished hard work, but I didn't relish cooking at such an early age however I've since learned to cook for my sons and my family. Even so, the experience made me a resourceful and pretty capable cook. I set a terrific table.

Food was not the topic of conversation at our table. Dinner was filled with nonstop talk of shipments, orders, invoices: the details of business. I sat, listened, and absorbed. Every meal was like a class.

At this point, my parents were understandably obsessed with business. Although my father was making a living in the lingerie business, he wasn't really established, and we remembered that everything could change overnight. For immigrants like us, financial stability and security seemed unattainable. My parents worked long hours every day, but they always managed to come home to eat meals with their children. Over the dinner table I responded for the first time to the excitement of business. But I believed my gender precluded me from running one. I believe this additional challenge can be a strong motivator for a woman entrepreneur. Despite my evident interest, it was an unspoken assumption that I would not end up a full-fledged businesswoman. It was understood, though, that my brother would become a businessman and I, a wife and mother.

We may have been living in the United States—in fact, my parents and I had become U.S. citizens in 1942, and my brother became a citizen while he was in the U.S. Army—but German discipline reigned in our household. We were expected to obey rules, no questions asked, no exceptions made. If we got bad grades, we knew we could look forward to stern words. My father was strict. But he was also kind and sympathetic, and he demonstrated his love and affection for me freely. I have fond memories of our evening strolls down Riverside Drive and Broadway: the whole family in a relaxed mood, meeting friends and stopping at Schrafft's for coffee and treats.

My mother was sparing in her praise and with her touch. To this day it haunts me, and I can't understand why. Her life as an immigrant was not easy. She had been accustomed to considerable wealth and a high social position, and that changed completely when she was forced to leave Germany. It was a difficult adjustment and may have contributed to her lack of personal warmth. She often made me unhappy with criticism that undermined my self-confidence and left me feeling inadequate. She frequently criticized my appearance, comparing my looks unfavorably to her own. I grew to feel that whatever went wrong was somehow my fault. In later years, if anything went amiss with my sons, I felt personally responsible. Now, however, I'm beginning to see light and security come in.

My mother could not understand how important it was for me to fit in with my peers. When the girls at school were wearing skirts and sweaters, cotton stockings and saddle shoes, she dressed me in garters, silk stockings, and starched blouses.

My doubts about my relationship with my mother were so strong that when I had an unpleasant and traumatic experience at the age of eleven, I didn't dare share it with her. I was sent to Hebrew school, and the rabbi who was my teacher ran his hand over my body. I was shattered. I told my brother and asked him whether he thought I should tell my mother. She knew I hated Hebrew lessons, and I was sure she wouldn't believe me. My brother concurred. Fortunately, that rabbi moved. Some years later, I told my mother what had happened, and she said that I should have told her, that of course she would have believed me. However, I knew I did the right thing.

I was unhappy at home during my adolescent years like many teenagers. I longed for a family that acted and spoke exactly like the families of the girls at school: a 100-percent American family. It wasn't until I was older that I appreciated how my upbringing, with one foot in the Old World and another in the New, added a valuable dimension to my life.

Hollywood as Berlitz

When I was fourteen, my father told me, "Lilly, you've got to earn your own money to pay for the extras." In my father's eyes, extras ranged from party dresses to dancing lessons, from lipstick to soda pop. My parents believed you had to work for possessions to truly appreciate them. So I started taking part-time jobs. My parents were right. There's pleasure and power in knowing that you've earned the money you hold in your hand and that you can spend it as you wish.

Just when we seemed finally settled, we suffered another family calamity. My father's business failed again. He was a stranger to American business methods and did not realize that he needed to hire a receptionist, a model, a secretary, a pattern maker, and a cutter. Those were costs his start-up company could not support. Once again, I saw him pick himself up. A week later, he was working as a dress salesman for one of his uncles. In a year, he had set up yet another business of his own, which once again he named Mercury Products Inc. He bought truckloads of old clothes to salvage the zippers, which were in short supply because of the war. He sold these zippers to ready-to-wear dress and suit manufacturers.

Resilience is an essential ingredient when running a business. I also learned that sometimes it's easier to start a new business than to keep a tired one going. I learned a lot during those years.

Fred and I spent every Saturday at our father's dusty loft on West Thirty-second Street, picking through mountains of filthy clothes, ripping out zippers. It was not my idea of fun, but no amount of hard work has ever dampened my spirits. Besides, I loved helping my father because he made me feel important.

Soon after, I began work as a salesclerk at Barton's candy store. There I discovered my sixth sense for other people's likes and tastes. I studied customers as they walked into the store, and by the time they reached the counter, I knew which candy to offer. I outsold all the other employees. I quit the job when I realized that Barton's generous free-sampling policy was adding all too generously to my figure.

Of all my jobs, my favorite was working as an usherette at the Riverside Movie Theater at Ninety-sixth and Broadway. It was one of those grand old movie palaces where there was a cartoon and a newsreel before the feature. Just showing up for work was glamorous. The pay was only twenty-five cents an hour, and our uniforms were used by other usherettes in several different shifts. But after the lights went down, I stood in the back and watched movie after movie. It was a marvelous education in all things American—most of all in the English language. Hollywood was my Berlitz.

My favorite film, *The Flight for Freedom—the Amelia Earhart Story*, starring Rosalind Russell, was truly inspirational. Amelia was a businesswoman as well as a courageous flyer and risk taker. I identified with her even though, at the time, I thought my prospects went no further than marriage and babies.

An Eye for Winners

As the war dragged on, old clothes became increasingly hard to come by. My enterprising father moved into the leather goods business—again naming his company Mercury Products. By that time, he was manufacturing in a loft on West Seventeenth Street, right around the corner from Barney's Men's Store. All the big leather companies were busy making products for the armed forces. My father produced small leather goods such as wallets, key cases, and pocket photograph holders. When peace came and well-established companies resumed production for the civilian market, he first switched to making camera cases for Kodak and then moved to making inexpensive copies of high-priced handbags for chain stores. The bags were his best sellers.

My mother shopped in Fifth Avenue department stores and selected the bags for him to copy, but her tastes were too European, too sophisticated. She liked ornate, ladylike items, more suitable for rich matrons.

One day, half jokingly, my father said to me, "Lillichen, why don't you go down to Fifth Avenue and bring me back some winners." Feeling grown-up and apprehensive, I went. The excitement I'd felt at Barton's candy store came back as I selected three handbags I just knew would be popular. They were simple, utilitarian, and youthful. To me they were the essence of American.

Indeed, they outsold anything else my father had made. He sent me out again, and I proved it was no fluke, repeating my success with other bags, wallets, and belts. Soon, I was my father's source. My success created more tension between my mother and me, because she liked to take credit for my choices. At the time, my shopping trips were simply another way to help the family. I never dreamed my skill would be the cornerstone of my career. What I recall most clearly was the feeling of self-worth and pride I experienced when I realized how valuable my instincts were, how I could trust them and act on them profitably.

Tragic Irony

My parents' attitude was an odd mixture of the modern and the old-fashioned: modern because they expected women to work and to succeed, and old-fashioned because they also expected them to marry and produce a family. There was no doubt that my father's real hopes and dreams were pinned on his son. Fred would be his successor. My father valued me, but he never considered me a possible partner.

While Fred was a sophomore at City College of New York, he was drafted into the U.S. Army. Because of his near-sighted eyes, he served as a medic in the Medical Corps.

Then the Army shipped Fred overseas to Europe. I fibbed about my age, and at seventeen, I joined a Women's Auxiliary Canteen. I worked for the war effort—handing out donuts to visiting servicemen. When I made a date with one serviceman, a well-meaning person took me aside to tell me that such behavior was forbidden. I believed I'd done nothing wrong: nobody had explained the rules.

It was an exciting and confusing time in the United States: a heady mix of sorrow and heroism, fear and hope. Every day we watched changing war maps in the newspapers. A neighbor's son was taken prisoner; another came home wounded; another was killed in action. The war brought back a renewed sense of life's fragility, and many social restraints disappeared in our determination to live for now, to seize the day.

We all lived for Fred's letters from Europe. Mail was irregular. Sometimes a week passed with no word, and then we would get three letters at once. After the Normandy invasion, three weeks passed without a letter. Then a month. Then a second month. We invented all sorts of reasons, but the unspoken was always on our minds.

I'll never forget the evening we learned the truth. My parents had quarreled at dinner, and my father had gone to the movies. I was in the shower when the doorbell rang. For no reason, the sound shot through my body like a bullet. I grabbed a robe and dashed into the living room. Mother stood there, holding a Western Union telegram. "I can't open it," she said softly. I took it from her hand, and we read it together. As of September 29, 1944, Fred was listed as missing in action in France. We didn't learn until April 19, 1945, that a grenade had killed him. The Germans had finished the job they started at the top of the stairway in Leipzig. That evening we called my uncle Jack, his wife, Sally, and our family doctor, Herman Kollon. When my father walked into the house and saw all of us gathered, he understood. Without a word spoken, he fainted. The doctor helped him, and my father claimed that he was fine, but to me he was never again the same person. A light had gone out of his life, and nothing would ever replace it. All the running, the struggling, the work had come down to this. He lost his zest for life and became vulnerable, lonely, and terribly, unalterably sad.

3

LOVE AND BUSINESS

A Honeymoon Discovery

—

A Dose of Reality

—

A Brainstorm

—

The Birth of a Trademark

—

Role Models—Where Were They?

—

A Great Moment

—

Suddenly I was the only child. My parents made it clear that I could no longer go off to college outside of New York City. I enrolled at New York University. Unlike City College of New York—CCNY, as it's commonly known—where Fred studied, New York University is not tuition-free. My parents were willing to pay the cost, twelve dollars per credit. Although I learned you don't necessarily need a college education to get ahead in life, I did profit a great deal from my years at NYU.

I studied with Sidney Hook, the prominent philosopher. I took courses in psychology and in American history and, just in case a husband was waiting for me somewhere, I also attended classes in home economics. After two years, I left NYU without a degree and went to work for my father. His business had done well during the war and prospered even more so afterward.

My parents planned a holiday weekend in 1949 at the Tisch Family Hotel in Lakewood, New Jersey. It was Washington's birthday. I didn't want to go, but they insisted. I still sometimes wonder what might have happened if I had stayed at home. Once there, I decided to make the best of it. I went to a dance at the hotel, and there I met Sam Hochberg. Sam introduced himself. I was wearing a short-sleeved party dress; Sam was a wonderful dancer.

That meeting shaped the course of my personal life—and my business life—for the next twenty years.

Sam was nine years my senior, a happy-go-lucky, charming, good-looking native New Yorker, born in Mount Vernon, New York, of Polish parents. He ran the family undergarments store in Mount Vernon. He was a CCNY graduate, as my brother would have been. Sam's love of sports and parties was a perfect complement to my energy and Germanic discipline. A large part of my attraction to him was that he was so different from my work-obsessed family. He brought out my fun-loving side, so long submerged by incessant work and the deep sadness of losing my brother.

By spring it was clear that we were in love, but Sam was in no hurry to propose. One cool, sunny May day my father took over, using a little not-so-subtle arm twisting. He took Sam for a walk and said, "I'm glad you and Lilly are getting married." Sam got the message.

Marriage, I believed, would give me the freedom I so longed for, but at the same time I had doubts about Sam. I noticed, for instance, that he would go off every afternoon to play tennis, leaving his mother to watch the store. To me, such behavior was inconceivable. I knew he loved tennis. But at the expense of his parents? When we were married, would I be left minding the store? Would he be able to support me? In the end, my father's enthusiasm overshadowed my doubts. He was so delighted at the prospect of seeing me married and settled, I felt I couldn't disappoint him. Ignoring my own misgivings, I went through with the marriage.

Our wedding preparations followed all the accepted social rules. We had a big engagement party in June. Our apartment was ablaze with beautiful bouquets sent by well-wishing friends. In September, we had a lavish wedding at the Astor Hotel on Broadway. And the bride wore white: a short-sleeved princess dress of satin, crowned with a long tulle veil. I loved every moment of the rituals of our Orthodox Jewish ceremony. We stood under the chuppah, I walked around the groom seven times, and Sam stamped on the glass wrapped in a linen napkin. The wedding was a family event. Relatives came from all over the world. I danced with Sam, with my father, with uncles and cousins, to the music of the big bands. For the first time, I—like every bride—felt like a star.

A Honeymoon Discovery

After the wedding, we flew to Bermuda, my first airplane ride. Bermuda was a wonderful place for me to honeymoon—and not just because of the pink sand and turquoise water. Bermuda allowed me to enjoy yet another first: with the money from wedding presents and the luxury of free time, I had the opportunity to wander through the shops of downtown Hamilton, selecting presents for friends and relatives. I was no longer merely observing other people's shopping. It was in Bermuda that I realized how much I really loved examining merchandise and trying to find the right gift for the right person. The whole process was an extension of what I'd learned in Amsterdam, at Barton's candy store, and in selecting handbags for my father's business. It was a creative outlet that employed my talents and my interests. Giving is an art: I had an eye for spotting the perfect item and the patience to keep looking until I found it.

Not long ago, I came across the letters that Sam and I wrote to my parents from Bermuda. Sam's gave an account of his daily athletic activities, mine described the romance and excitement of the island. The letters summed up the different ways we experienced our honeymoon, and foreshadowed the dynamics of our marriage.

A Dose of Reality

In 1949, the country was still mired in a postwar housing shortage. Sam and I were lucky to find a modest furnished apartment on the top floor of a Tudor house in Mount Vernon, a pleasant suburb of New York City. It consisted of three rooms in what had probably once been maids' quarters. The ceilings were low and slanted and really fun.

I loved fixing it up, transforming it into a handsome home with contemporary furniture. I remember all I bought and all I needed to make my first home. I spent hours moving furniture around so that our armchair was displayed to its best advantage and created a welcoming and comfortable atmosphere.

Sam and I were happy there—once we learned to duck our heads. The apartment had the added advantage, especially for Sam, of being quite near Hochberg's Dry Goods Store, one of his family's two haberdashery shops. Sam worked there, making $75 a week. Once we had paid the rent, the car payment, and taxes, there wasn't enough for the extras that make life fun. So I took part-time jobs. I got my daily house chores down to twelve minutes flat, which left seven hours and forty-eight minutes for more profitable work. I sold pots and pans by phone. I kept the books at a textile company. I sold dresses at Lerner Shops, a popular women's clothing chain. I worked on commission and seemed to sell the most. Wherever I worked, I kept my eyes and ears open and tried to learn something about what makes a business work—or fail.

As young marrieds, Sam and I had great times together. Leading the life expected of a young wife, I played canasta with young women friends, most of whom were either pregnant or already mothers. Sam played tennis with his athletic pals. With our mutual friends, we played as much as we could afford to, sampling everything from the humor and risqué dances found at clubs in Hoboken, New Jersey, to the exciting professionalism of the Broadway stage.

In 1951, I got pregnant. I knew we would need a larger place and more income, but in those days, a pregnant woman was supposed to devote herself exclusively to the baby she was carrying. Hovering in the background was always the accepted idea that a working wife was an embarrassing commentary on her husband's earning power.

It didn't occur to me then to question this attitude. I probably voiced many of the same biased sentiments myself. Even so, I could read the numbers. It was a dilemma: I had to earn money, but I couldn't leave the house.

A Brainstorm

Restless and anxious, with empty hours to fill, I sat at our yellow Formica kitchen table—everyone had one of them—and, through the window, watched the seasons change. In the distance trains went back and forth from the suburbs to New York City. Today, the sound of a train whistle always takes me back to that chrome-legged kitchen table and the early anxious days. I spent a lot of time flipping through magazines like *Seventeen*, *Glamour*, and *Charm*. It wasn't the articles that intrigued me so much as the ads in the shopping columns. Which of the items would I buy if I had the money? One morning as I sat sipping coffee and eating a mother-to-be breakfast, leafing through the magazines in my usual back-to-front fashion, I was struck with an idea. Why couldn't I sell something through the mail, out of my home? What could be more natural, logical, and profitable? I would be using my experience and the skills I had acquired picking out handbags for my father, buying gifts in Bermuda, observing shoppers in many places. I knew, instinctively, that I would love such an undertaking.

From that moment, I felt a sense of purpose. I knew where I wanted to put my energy and my passion, and I felt a sense of inadequacy (a common thread among young people trying to find their way in life) begin to pass. Miraculously, the feelings I had battled gave way to the new sensation of self-confidence.

I brooded over my alternatives, examining the various angles. I would invest some of our wedding-present money—$2,000. I prayed that Sam and my parents would approve.

Full of excitement, I told Sam my plan.

"You're going to put an ad in a woman's magazine?" he asked.

"Yes," I said. "I can run the whole business without leaving the apartment."

START-UP EXPENSES

No matter what business you're in—even if you work at home—you will have start-up costs. Keep them to a bare minimum, but anticipate your expenditures and formulate an initial budget. Plan for increases in all your expenses. Before long you will probably need a second phone. A prerequisite for any business, no matter how small, is an answering machine. You will have to buy supplies and equipment for making your product or delivering your service. Expect your gasoline costs to rise. It's important not to become over-enthusiastic: be cautious about building inventories until you are certain of your sales potential. You will have to order stationery and business cards, but don't get fancy. You may have advertising costs, even if you take advantage of your local newspaper's relatively low rates. If you need lawyers and accountants, don't forget to factor their fees into your budget. And you will have to take out at least some insurance as a hedge against disaster, so you must not forget the cost of those premiums. Don't expect to begin a viable mail-order business with less than $100,000 to $250,000 in your cash kitty. Check out the business you want to enter for start-up costs. They probably won't be much different from those for starting a mail-order business.

Sam grinned. "What are you going to sell, Lilly?"

"I don't know. I'll think of something."

That night, my mind was racing and my heart pounding. I would be my own woman, and I knew I could make a success of anything I undertook. No doubt about it, Herman Menasche's daughter had inherited her father's determination and his optimism.

The Birth of a Trademark

In my first two years of marriage, I produced a son and a business.

One afternoon in early 1951, as I was walking restlessly through my father's plant in midtown Manhattan, my business plan solidified. Handbags. I knew about those, why not sell them, and belts to match? Didn't every teenage girl strolling along the street, anywhere in the United States, sport a handbag and belt? And my handbags would offer something special: each one would be personalized with the owner's initials. I knew with absolute certainty that teenagers would go for items that made them feel unique—as long as their peers had them, too. What I didn't yet know was that I'd hit upon an idea that would become my trademark. Monogramming!

I believe that this idea, and my instinctive understanding of its appeal, grew out of my childhood experiences as a stranger in many lands. I knew well the longing both to belong and to stand out.

The first step was finding the right styles of bags and belts to personalize. They had to fit my image of a teenager's taste. Before placing the ad, I turned to my father for help. He was going to be my supplier. One afternoon, my father and I walked through his factory studying the purses and belts.

"They're all beautiful," I said, "but not quite right. I want something really special."

My father seemed hurt at first, but only for a moment.

"You want really special, Lilly? We'll make you one that's really special."

For the next three hours, I described my ideas while my father sketched rough designs. I saw the bag as petite—to convey a neat and stylish image—with a shoulder strap and a heraldic metal crest on the front. The initials were to go on the strap. The wide, waist-cincher belt would buckle in back and have a tab on the front for initials that matched those on the bag—the first matching bag and belt set ever!

To this day the smell of raw leather and saddle oil conjures up the image of my father sitting at his drawing board, his talented hands giving shape to my thoughts. He never treated me as anything less than an equal, and from that I learned a lot!

While my father unwaveringly supported my plan, my mother and Sam were just the opposite. Both thought I was nuts and didn't hesitate to tell me.

"You know nothing about business," Sam pointed out.

"You can't even type properly," my mother added. "You've never used an adding machine."

I was surprised by my mother's opposition. She, after all, had been a working woman all her life. How could she take me to task for doing the same? Still, I was determined to follow my plan. Now that I had discovered what to sell, the next question was how to sell it.

I decided to run an ad in *Seventeen*, a magazine aimed at the teenage market. After weeks of agonizing over the perfect product to offer, I now agonized over every word of the ad. I read my efforts to Sam and to my father, and consulted other people I trusted. Finally I was satisfied. The copy read, "Be First to Sport the Personalized Look on Your Bag and Belt." It was simple, direct, and alluring.

With the bag designed, I faced some difficult arithmetic. How much should I charge? Producing the bag and the belt cost $1.50, and I had to add shipping costs to that. My father's time had to be compensated, and I certainly had to profit from my business, no matter how small. My father and I figured it out together. We had to charge a $0.60 federal war tax on the bag but no tax on the belt. We discussed a price of $3.00 for the bag and $2.00 for the belt. That sounded a little expensive, but $2.95 and $1.95 might not cover our costs. We compromised with $2.99 and $1.99. Every penny counted.

It's hard to describe the satisfaction I felt as I immersed myself in work. It was a feeling of control, of creativity, of self-worth. How many hundreds of times have people said they admire my ability to work hard. Only rarely do I reveal my secret: for me, work is fun and always has been.

Role Models—Where Were They?

When I first broached my project, even my father, helpful as he was, thought I shouldn't begin while I was pregnant. I had to convince him that I could handle everything. (How wrong I was. I couldn't do quite everything.)

In those days, having a baby was like having a disease. Women stayed in the hospital for ten days. Some men were skittish about even uttering the word *pregnant*.

Most people assumed that a pregnant woman was not going to work. Once, when I was standing on the sidewalk and trying to hail a taxi, a man—no doubt he saw himself as a knight in shining armor—came up and offered to take me to the hospital. I was very pregnant. He was taken aback when I told him I was only on my way to work. When I think of what women had to put up with, I wonder how we did it. Things are better today, but still there's only one woman at the helm of a Fortune 500 company, Linda Wachner of Warnaco.

Women need role models, and even today they are hard to find. In the 1950s, when I began my business, there were none—not in the magazine stories we read, the movies we saw, or the novels we purchased. A businesswoman was considered—by men and women alike—unfeminine. Worse, a working woman was a rude intruder in a man's world. To describe a man as tough was to compliment him, but to call a woman tough was to insult her. The message was, "Be content as a wife, mother, secretary, teacher, or nurse." Those women who worked in a business usually worked for their husbands. True, a few well-established companies were owned or run by women: Dorothy Shaver headed Lord &

Taylor, Elizabeth Arden and Helena Rubinstein founded successful cosmetic companies, Coco Chanel was a prominent fashion designer, Miriam Haskell designed jewelry. But those businesses—cosmetics, fashion, and jewelry—were aimed at women. While it was—and is—true that mail-order customers are mostly women, men owned and ran those businesses. So there I was, moving into a man's world.

It never occurred to me that I was trespassing on male territory, stepping into a potentially hostile world. My spirit prevailed and I moved ahead.

A Great Moment

In the sweltering New York summer of 1951, I was obsessed with two dates: September 1, when I would launch the Vernon Specialties Company with my modest ad for monogrammed products, and February 3, when my baby was due. I had gambled $495 of our $2,000 wedding-gift nest egg (venture capital, today) on the first ad, which was to run in *Seventeen*'s September issue. In mid-August, I started hounding the man at the corner newsstand.

"Lady, the September magazines aren't out yet," he said. "I'll save you a copy. I'll save you ten copies."

I was four months pregnant, but I walked up and down the street in the heat, sheepishly checking other newsstands, just in case. I had no idea that one tiny ad would change my life as much as the tiny baby growing inside me.

When the September issue of *Seventeen* finally arrived, I bought twelve copies and stood there flipping the pages to find my little one-sixth-of-a-page ad. I cried as I looked at it. It had seemed so grand on the drawing board, but seeing it on the page, competing with slick illustrated ads for make-up, clothes, and acne medicines, I wondered whether anyone would notice.

I projected a profit of $1,000. Estimating that I had put

in about 2,000 hours of work, I figured I would make $0.50 an hour. I didn't care. It was my own business. The truth is, a $50 profit would have pleased and inspired me—and launched me into the mail-order world.

"What if the ad doesn't pull?" Sam asked when I showed it to him. "What if we lose it all?" His skepticism and negativity were typical.

For the next few days, I was a nervous wreck. I couldn't sit still—even at my kitchen table/desk. The world was in slow motion, and I was revved up like a sports car. I kept flipping through *Seventeen*, imagining I was a teenager in Omaha or a young woman in New Orleans admiring hairstyles and fall clothes. My imaginary reader would soon have a wedding, followed by eager young motherhood. I understood her secret dreams and could fantasize with her. In Germany, as a child, I had been ostracized. In Holland, I was teased for being German. In the United States, I was an immigrant who could not speak English. In a strange way, I was offering my customers the security and self-confidence in their growing years that I had lacked.

Finally, Sam called from his store, the address we had given in the ad.

"Did we get an order?"

"No," he said. "We got fifty."

From that moment, my life was changed forever.

4

THE TAKE-OFF

The Entrepreneur

—

Experimenting

—

The Baby and the Business

—

Orders poured in—$16,000 in the first six weeks, a miraculous $32,000 before the end of the year. Altogether, I received orders for 6,450 bags and belts. That little ad proved to be pure poetry. Never again in the history of my mail-order business has a single ad brought such a phenomenal response. It first appeared in *Seventeen*'s back-to-school issue, and it seemed to me that every teenage girl in the United States wanted to hop out of the school bus wearing her own personalized belt, carrying her own personalized bag. Though I was thrilled at the success, I was too busy to take time out to celebrate.

The highlight of every day was the arrival of the mail. I'd sit at my kitchen table and get to work. It was slow going at first, but before long, I was zipping through one hundred pieces of mail an hour. I piled the orders on one side and the checks, money orders, and cash on the other. I typed address labels, banging at the old typewriter keys with two fingers.

When the mail was done, I took the train into New York and worked in my father's factory, embossing every item with the appropriate gold initials. Then I packed each order and hauled it to the post office.

"Mrs. Hochberg, you're in the home stretch. Try to take it a little easy," my doctor admonished me. "Remember that even God rested on the seventh day. Take a seventh-inning stretch, and take it every day!"

I was feeling too strong, happy, even omnipotent, to pay much attention. One day a friend saw me lugging three fifty-pound mailbags from my car to the post office. "Lilly, are you crazy?" she shrieked at me. "You're pregnant. Why isn't Sam doing that?"

I just smiled. Sam was working at the store. I would have hauled twenty sacks, and often I did.

When Sam heard about the encounter, he bawled me out. He Tarzan, me Jane. I did cut back, but every once in a while, when he wasn't around, I took the bags to the post office anyway. I loved it. I loved every mundane detail of the business.

I couldn't afford an adding machine, but I had nerve. I asked my friendly banker in Mount Vernon for help. Even now I remember greeting him politely as "Mr. Baker." If he had a first name, I was too much in awe to use it. Of course, he never would have given me a loan, but every Friday morning I went to the bank and he allowed me to sit at a corner of his desk and use his adding machine.

Without being consciously aware of it, I was absorbing the basic ABCs of the mail-order business: get the product, advertise it to the right audience, take your orders, package them, and ship them out. Sounds simple, doesn't it? At that point, I'd fooled myself into thinking it would always be so straightforward and matter-of-fact. I was blissfully unaware of the unexpected demands, complications, and crises that would crop up as my business grew.

The Entrepreneur

I was only twenty-two, and although I was far from realizing it then, I had become a true entrepreneur. Back then, I saw it as a case of plain common sense: I needed cash, and I had figured out how to make money in a way that fit my circumstances.

If I had not been endowed with an entrepreneurial spirit, I might have sat at home and felt sorry for myself as I fretted about finances. Inactivity and self-pity are alien to me! People describe entrepreneurs as resourceful, passionate about what they do, imaginative, even visionary. They are inventors and innovators. I constantly hear that they are risk takers. Personally, I don't believe that entrepreneurs ever think of risks. Instead, we have confidence in our ideas and

CASH

From the day you start your business, you must keep track of your cash. If you have the time, take classes and read books that teach you how to budget. A computer with a budget program—no matter how simple—can help you, or you can buy yourself a ledger and do it by hand. In both cases, be sure you make your entries every day.

What you should aim for is *liquidity,* the business world's term for actual cash. There are misunderstandings about the word *cash;* profits are not cash, accounts receivable are not cash until they are received, and physical assets are not cash. Although your computer system is a company asset, it can't pay the utility bills or meet your employees' salaries. Think of cash for your company as you think of the money in your checking account: it is always available. You use it to pay bills, to tide you over in an emergency: suppose a labor strike hits your product-delivery system and you can't get the goods to the customer on time. Once your business is established, only cash can give you the wherewithal to expand.

There is another point to be made about cash; it takes some time to arrive. Suppose you paid off your bills for inventory and you have sold enough product to show, on paper anyway, a profit. Until your customers actually pay you, however, you have no cash on hand. There may be a time lag ranging from two to three months between your outlay and your cash income. That is the harrowing time for a beginning business.

decisions. That is true of me. One of the most exciting aspects of being an entrepreneur is being in a position to make situations work for you. You have taken what many would consider a risk—maybe a big risk—and it succeeds. You have transformed a disadvantage into an advantage through your own ideas and your own hard work.

It's possible that I inherited the entrepreneurial spirit, that it was a gift, from my mother's great-grandfather. As a young man, he left Cracow, Poland, and emigrated to Antwerp, Belgium. There, in 1860, he helped found the diamond business, an industry that grew until Antwerp became its world headquarters. He must have been an entrepreneur par excellence.

My father's family, too, likely had a hand in my entrepreneurial makeup. In my father's family, the example came through the women. His mother raised four of her own sons and an orphaned cousin while she ran the family business. Her husband was an orthodox Rabbi with a long white beard. Like my mother's family, my father's had emigrated from Poland to Germany and done well there. My mother was envious of her mother-in-law, whose sons adored her, and I have always felt that Oma Menasche's character has come down to me. She was a hardworking, strong-minded, determined, and goal-oriented woman. She was difficult at times, as am I.

Both my parents came from families that had done well in business. I'm sure that pogroms originally drove them out of Poland, but once they were in Western Europe, they prospered and moved—financially at least—into the upper class. Socially, Polish Jews were not accepted in Germany, not even by German Jews.

Whatever valuable attributes I may have inherited from my forebears, they were immeasurably enhanced by a course in American history I took at New York University. The course taught me never to accept the conventional interpretation of the past or, by extension, the present. On the opening day of class, our American history professor, Dr. Thomas

Cochrane, announced that by examining both sides, and ana-lyzing the relationship between cause and effect, we would understand that history can be interpreted in many ways. Some of our most dearly held assumptions were not neces-sarily so, he said. That professor taught me a lesson I'll never forget: Always look beyond conventional interpretations and the obvious. His influence has stayed with me all my life, and the Lillian Vernon endowment of a chair at NYU is my way of paying back a debt I have always felt I owed.

The university educated me and helped me in my life's work, just as it did for my son Fred. This chair is endowed with love and respect for what my teachers gave me. I believe so strongly in the value of international studies that I also helped establish the NYU Global House, which supports students from countries throughout the world.

From the very first, I loved my work because it was mine, because I had created it. To this day, it thrills me when I come up with an idea that pays off. Look at it this way: If your busi-ness stops making money, it stops breathing. But you don't live your life just to keep breathing. You live it for a sense of accomplishment, of satisfaction.

During that autumn of 1951, I knew I had accomplished something. I still felt overwhelmed and unprepared. I knew that if I were to achieve all I aimed for, I faced a long, chal-lenging road. Life was not going to be chocolate-covered cherries in a Baccarat bowl.

Experimenting

Seventeen had worked beyond all expectations. Perhaps *Charm* and *Glamour* would work for me, too. I was wrong. Orders merely dribbled in. "How about *Vogue*?" I asked Sam. "Let's spend $400 and see what happens."

He gave me a look I was to see many times. It said, "Lillian, you're a gambler who doesn't know when to stop." My warning to all entrepreneurs: When you see that look, turn away and ignore it. I wish I knew how to do that without giving offense, but I never learned. Perhaps it isn't possible.

I spent a lot of my early profits on ads that failed, in *Town and Country* and *Harper's Bazaar*, for instance. But in addition to losing money, I learned a valuable business lesson. I discovered a fundamental rule of merchandising: Know your market. I had picked a bag and belt especially suited to the tastes of teenagers. What was I doing, advertising in magazines like *Vogue* that catered to an entirely different readership? Still, we made enough to keep going. Every time I got discouraged, I'd visit my father.

"Lilly," he said, "we came to America with nothing. We didn't even know the language. Remember? Now I've managed to start and keep a good business afloat. To begin with, there were a lot of false starts, and there was a lot of hard work. So you mustn't let a few minor mistakes discourage you. Keep going, and I know you'll come out on top. If you do that, success will be yours forever!"

Today, I realize that I would have had it easier with a business plan, some elementary economics courses behind me, and a basic knowledge of accounting. I relied instead on what I had learned from those dinner-table conversations between my parents. They taught me the language of business. If you don't have access to such home tutoring, my advice is: Prepare yourself before spending money on your idea.

Meanwhile, our small Mount Vernon apartment was growing cluttered with file boxes and papers. And once a week, I lumbered off to use my banker's adding machine. I was growing bigger every day.

The Baby and the Business

After that Christmas rush of 1951, I took a breather. Not a long one: on February 3, I gave birth to a splendid eight-pound, two-ounce boy. We named him Fred Philip, after my brother and my mother's father. He had my brother's dark hair, and I thought that he looked like him. Every mother knows the incomparable sense of achievement that comes from bearing a child. I had borne a business at the same time. I experienced a double dose of elation. What a year it had been. Would I have gone ahead if I had known what kind of hard work and responsibility there would be? Absolutely.

5

LEADING A DOUBLE LIFE

Juggling, Anyone?

—

Out into the Business World, at Last

—

Branching Out

—

A Valuable Lesson

—

Lillian Vernon Is Born

—

It was good that I loved my business because looking after it and caring for my baby took lots of time and energy.

Every night, when Fred fell asleep, I'd whip out my customer order forms and sit at the typewriter, organizing them. I made endless lists of customers, their orders, the inventory warehoused at my father's factory, products that had to be ordered, goods that had to be shipped. I've always been a list maker and an organizer. Here I was with diapers in the tub, dishes in the sink, and order forms—everywhere! Because I'm a neatnik, I have always been frustrated and unsettled by the disorder, but I had to do everything myself—including putting Sam's meals on the table. Young and crazy—filled with such energy!

One reason women make such great managers in business is that they have experience dealing with multiple distractions. Time management is an invaluable skill, and I honed mine running a household and a business simultaneously. Once you've dressed a struggling infant in a snowsuit, argued about the gas bill, and composed an enticing ad—all while the meatloaf bakes in the oven—the rest is a breeze. The harder I worked, the more fun it was. There were times I was exhausted. Whenever that happened, one of my father's favorite sayings came to mind: "If it were easy, anyone could do your job." The memory of those words always revived my enthusiasm back into my work. There wasn't enough money to hire a helper, and Sam was busy at his family's store. I simply had to run the business. It was my hard-work ethic that helped me to survive. When I felt my head nodding I would sit up and say, "This must get done."

More ads in *Seventeen* followed, offering handbags and belts in three different colors. I kept careful, up-to-date records on 3"-by-5" index cards: the names and addresses of customers, what they had ordered, and when. Ultimately, that record became the foundation of the Lillian Vernon Corporation.

Juggling, Anyone?

"Busy-ness" was great training for my future. The fiction was that my business was strictly a sideline, a hobby.

"Don't overdo it," Sam said. "Remember, you're just trying to make a few extra dollars and keep yourself occupied."

I had ambitions, but I kept them hidden, even from myself. It was a secret part of me, which I didn't share with anyone. I was afraid to reveal the depth of my determination to succeed. It was after all the early 1950s. Rosie the Riveter of World War II days had in most instances turned in her welding torch for a waffle iron. Few married women with children went off to a job. If I had worked full-time, in the open, people would have thought Sam was doing badly or that my child was neglected. A lot of women suppressed their natural abilities then. Some women still do so today. "I'm just trying to make a few dollars and keeping occupied."

When Fred was a baby, I was home most of the time. When I had to go into the city to work in my father's factory, I hired my baby-sitter, Odele. As soon as I could, in came the cleaning woman for five dollars to work half a day every Friday. My Germanic upbringing may have made me hardworking, but it did not turn me into the classic German do-it-all hausfrau. Far from it. I'm too practical to ignore a sensible distribution of responsibility.

My eagerness to spend hours at my business didn't mean I didn't take pride in being a wife and a mother. I discovered how much joy motherhood brought, what great pleasures a child brings. On the other hand, I grew up with nannies, so the idea of other women caring for Fred—and later, David—during working hours didn't seem unreasonable, unloving, or neglectful.

From the first, though, I ran into unspoken opposition. Essentially, my mother and Sam didn't think my work was serious. They humored me. My mother refused to baby-sit when I needed to go to a gift show in Atlantic City.

"You belong with your child," she said flatly. "I don't belong being your child's sitter."

Her judgmental attitude never really changed.

Successful businesswomen were few and far between in those days. For years, no one would extend me credit: I always had to pay cash. A few times I had to order extra shipping boxes in a hurry. When I asked for short-term credit, the response was always "Not possible." The cruelest blows followed my miscarriages in 1953 and 1954. Even when the doctors assured me that those pregnancies had been problematic due to medical complications beyond my control, people—even my closest relatives—implied that I had lost the babies because I worked.

Out into the Business World, at Last

Despite setbacks, the business grew at a good pace. Finally, I accumulated so many customer files that our kitchen could no longer house them. By chance, there was an empty room behind Sam's store. Although it was only fourteen feet square, it was big enough to hold a desk, a chair, and my filing cabinets. I was proud of my first genuine office. I also rented a nearby storefront for shipping orders, and I hired part-time help. Some of those part-timers were my girlfriends, and it didn't take all that long before I discovered how unwise this was. Business and friendship aren't necessarily compatible. I got someone to help me at home when I needed more help. I split my days between the office and the house. And twice a week, I visited my father's factory to do the initialing and packaging.

Shopping centers were sprouting up around downtown Mount Vernon, and Sam's haberdashery was languishing. One night over dinner I said delicately, "Sam, have you thought about coming into my business full time?"

Sam took another bite and ignored my question. I repeated it.

Finally, he pursed his lips and said, "Lillian, my business is doing $40,000 a year. When your business does more than $40,000 a year, we'll talk."

In 1954, my sales hit $41,000. I mentioned it again.

"Well, Sam?" I asked.

Sam reluctantly left his parents' store and joined the company as president, at $100 a week. I became vice president, at $50. I took Sam's higher salary for granted. All my life, I had been brainwashed to accept a discrepancy between a man's and a woman's earnings. When I think about it now, I really wonder. I once heard former Mayor of New York City Ed Koch say that a woman's brain deserved the same respect and the same pay as a man's. I agree.

One day when I was at my father's factory, he offered me his customary sound business advice.

"Lilly, I have two words for you: diversify and diversify."

"But everything I sell, I buy from you. I couldn't be disloyal."

"I want you to learn to think. To consider all possibilities. Suppose I have a bad year? Besides, I won't be around forever."

Although I couldn't imagine life without him, my father was right. I had to branch out. The opportunity to grow was available, and we could not afford to stand still.

Branching Out

I went to Providence, Rhode Island, to my first jewelry show. I found all sorts of gold-plated pins, rings, cuff links, and lockets to add to my monogrammed line. Soon I was selling to adults through such magazines as *House Beautiful* and *Better Homes and Gardens.*

That's when I found one of my all-time most popular products—one we've continued to sell for forty-six years. It was a monogrammed bookmark: the price was $1, three for $2.75. To sell it, we advertised in magazines aimed at an adult market; no point in selling a bookmark to teenagers. We placed ads in *Redbook, House and Garden, Glamour,* and

---

YOUR PRODUCT OR SERVICE

The foundation of your future business success is your product or service. You must offer something that people want to buy. You'll gather ideas as you work, chat with friends, garden, watch children play, drive, watch television, and, shop. It is a good investment of your time to browse through shops, street fairs, and offbeat little boutiques. Wherever you find yourself and whatever you are doing, keep your mind open to ideas for products or services that might satisfy needs. Also watch for ways to improve what is already on the market. My emphasis has always been on the words *special* and *exclusive*. There were plenty of belts and bags for teenagers to choose from when I started my business, but my belts and bags were distinctive because I monogrammed them.

One expert has described mail order as the business of ideas. I would say that the same is true of all businesses today.

similar publications. We were aiming for a more sophisticated audience. When we first advertised it, I was in the hospital awaiting David's birth. I was hospitalized during the three weeks preceding his birth on October 22, 1956. When the bookmark ad broke, in *Redbook* on October 1, we sold about 20,000—a phenomenon we didn't repeat until 1957. I didn't even know about the sales. I wasn't at the center of all the excitement. However, I used our profits from the bookmark to expand our line once again. We advertised combs, blazer buttons, collar pins with matching cuff links,

---

ACCOUNTANTS AND LAWYERS

For an entrepreneur with some cash, hiring an accountant and consulting a lawyer are often worthwhile. Accountants with small-business experience can advise you about the best structure for your venture: partnership, sole proprietorship, S corporation, or C corporation. They'll show you how to estimate and track your start-up expenses as well as how to forecast your breakeven point.

Your lawyer will guide you through the legal and regulatory mazes that challenge all businesses: these range from local zoning ordinances to the federal rules that govern your industry. You can possibly contend with all of that yourself, but you will find it an onerous burden that is time-consuming. If given a choice, most entrepreneurs would rather put their time and energy into their product or service.

In the end, advice from professionals will save you money. Don't be afraid to ask for payment terms that you can handle. As a beginner, you can cut a good deal and have the promise of good business to come.

and even golden toothpicks: and we monogrammed everything.

We took another step away from the purely teenage market, expanding into such consumer goods as towels, and sold those products through magazines that homemakers liked to read. I had learned my lesson when I tried to sell teenagers' bags and belts to readers of *Vogue*, and was now careful to match the product with the market.

For the first time I found myself dealing with businesspeople in the marketplace. Most men I met on my trips to Providence—and they were always men—were not only good company but also full of useful information. More than once, Sam said, with perhaps a touch of jealousy, "How come you're so charming to all those guys?" What could I say? I loved all they had to teach me.

A Valuable Lesson

The truth is, I was getting a crash course in reality. I learned one salutary lesson early on.

I'll never forget Richard Meyers. He was a likable fellow with a ready joke and a warm smile who wanted to sell our bags and belts on commission in his catalog. When he got an order, we filled it and paid him the commission. His orders poured in. They were all C.O.D.—cash on delivery. What looked too good to be true turned out to be just that. Our genial con man had invented the orders, and on top of the commission, we ended up paying double the C.O.D. charges when the packages came back to us. Dick Meyers had even gone so far as to give me a fatherly warning about unscrupulous characters. He must have been talking about himself. Think twice before you give your trust, and maintain a healthy skepticism at all times.

Despite the setbacks, the business grew fast through the decade of the 1950s. Despite our success, I still followed my basic rule of thumb: invest like a Rockefeller, live like a pauper. I was running the company like a French housewife—no leftovers. I recycled paper clips, used the backs of order forms for scratch pads, and composed copy on a $25 manual typewriter. We laboriously cranked out our mailing labels on an old Addressograph. And we always reinvested in the business—mainly in increased advertising. If there's a single piece of advice I can give new entrepreneurs, it is: take as little money as possible out of the business. We took enough to eat, live, and educate our children. The rest went back into building the business. In 1955 our revenues were $155,000. In 1956 they reached $195,000, and I reinvested somewhere between $25,000 and $30,000 of that in the company. Just as real estate people tell you that location, location, and location are the three essential considerations when buying a house, so do I believe that reinvest, reinvest, and reinvest are the three basic rules of starting up a business and keeping it going. I still reinvest. There's a line in Thornton Wilder's play *The Matchmaker* to the effect that money is like manure, it should be used to make things grow. If I invest in someone else's company, I'm investing in other people's management. I prefer to put my money into my own company. That's the best way to maintain control and make a profit.

Lillian Vernon Is Born

When Sam and I began to work together, we didn't really coordinate too well. At first we both signed checks, and as a result we got a lot of phone calls thanking us for sending two payments. As you can imagine, we straightened that out pretty fast. It became my job to monitor the bills and to sign checks.

The time had come to incorporate. In 1960, we registered the name Vernon Specialties Inc., but discovered that another company—a paint solvent manufacturer—had already registered that name in New York State. So we renamed our company Vernon Products, Inc. Five years later, we introduced the Lillian Vernon Corporation. After all, 99 percent of our customers were women. I liked my American name, Lillian, and we had built the business in Mount Vernon. Now I prefer my real name, Lilly.

The 1950s was a heady decade in which to launch a mail-order business. We may never again see the optimism of those Eisenhower years. The country was exploding with energy and possibilities. And money. Who thought it would ever end? After the austerity of the 1930s and 1940s, people loved to spend. Please, they seemed to be saying, give us something to buy. I was more than happy to oblige.

My partnership with Sam became a double one. We shared family life and business expansion. The bookmark, which sold so well, contributed wonderfully to our growth, but everything we offered our customers sold well. Obviously, the business arrangement between Sam and me was working well.

THE STRUCTURE OF YOUR BUSINESS

ONE OWNER

Of your choices for your business, by far the simplest is sole proprietorship. You alone own the business. There are no shares, and there is no division of potential profits. You call the shots: you decide how to spend your cash, how to manage your time, and how to sell your products or services. Financial liability is the chief drawback to this arrangement. Should your business fail, you can lose everything you own—cash reserves, house, car, and furniture— to pay off your debts. A sole proprietor cannot legally file for Chapter 11 bankruptcy protection.

PARTNERSHIP

This arrangement is relatively easy to set up, but you will need a lawyer to draw up an agreement that protects your interests. A partner can bring much-needed cash, experience, and support into the fledgling business. With a partner, you have someone with whom you can discuss problems, map out strategy, and formulate goals. A partnership, unlike a corporation, is not liable to double taxation. The owners aren't subject to a separate corporate income tax. So any profit that you do not reinvest in your business is divided between you and your partner. Just be absolutely certain before you enter into a partnership that your capabilities complement each other and that you can work well together. Like a sole proprietorship, a partnership leaves you and your partner personally liable for debts.

If you find that your partnership is not working out as you hoped it would, then it can be dissolved by conducting a buyout or closing the business.

INCORPORATION

A corporation is a distinct legal entity with limited liability. Should you decide to retire or to sell, you can transfer ownership by selling shares, and the corporation will continue to exist without you. The type of corporate structure you choose for your business— S corporation or C corporation—will have a distinct impact on your tax status. If you form an S corporation, you avoid double taxation. In other words, the corporation does not pay taxes. You pay taxes on any monies you take out of the company as income for yourself. A C corporation pays taxes directly.

Forming a corporation can be a complex and expensive procedure that calls for expert legal advice. Someone beginning a business with only meager financing may want to postpone forming a corporation until the business is established.

6

LEARNING THE JEWELRY BUSINESS

Meeting a Mentor

—

A Big Hit

—

My Golden Gut

—

On the Lookout

—

Flare-ups

—

Family Life

—

In 1956, personal and professional life converged: my second son, David, arrived on October 22, just as the Christmas rush was beginning, and I set into work again. I didn't mind one bit. After the heartbreak of two miscarriages, this birth seemed to be a true miracle.

Early in 1957, I decided to branch out again. We had been buying our jewelry ready-made from a manufacturer in Providence. That changed when I discovered that he was outrageously overcharging me: he charged $4.50 a dozen for items I could make for $2.25 a dozen. "Enough of that," I said to Sam. "Let's make our own."

Sam: "But we don't know anything about manufacturing jewelry."

Me: "We'll learn."

The assumption was that we could produce our own bracelets and necklaces at a substantial savings. Given what I knew, it was a reasonable assumption. I was blithely innocent of the complications involved. Jewelry manufacturing follows an intricate path from design to final product. There are many steps along the way where it's easy to make serious mistakes. I soon discovered that jewelry manufacturing demands careful and constant supervision.

Meeting a Mentor

Once again, my luck held. I went to Providence for a show and to investigate the business. There I discovered Marty Waxman. We met through a manufacturer who told him it might be worth his while to talk to me. Marty was working for an electro-plating company, making $100 a week. I asked him if he would work for me as an expediter. His boss said that as long as he did it on his own time, he had no objections, as long as we used him as our plater. Marty's job was to make sure that every item moved without difficulty through every complex step of manufacturing. We did everything on contract: from casting—we did our own designs—to brass stamping, to soldering or welding, and then, finally, to plating in gold or silver. Marty had to make certain that every item stayed on schedule. It was an important and demanding job.

Marty and I hit it off right away. He was a good-natured, intensely loyal man, who had started as an upholsterer and switched over to jewelry. He was amiable and towering—six-feet–four-inches tall—with an open face. I never failed to be charmed by his quick wit. He was also one of the most enterprising people I have ever worked with. A few years after we started working together we had a contract with Revlon, the cosmetic giant. Revlon submitted an order that had to be filled immediately. And Revlon accepted no excuses. It was midsummer and so hot that all the jewelry plating plants had shut down. What did Marty do? He went out to Quonset Point where the Navy was stationed and talked some of the young men there into coming to his plating plant to help get the job done. They worked all night, and Revlon got its order on time.

Marty was my friend and we remained close until his death in 1988. I knew Marty over thirty years and still miss him today. Our friendship was so close that Marty sometimes teased Sam by saying, "I'm your partner in marriage." That usually came after I had complained to Marty that an order was late, or some such problem. Sam would tease back, "You're the only other man who knows what it's like to be married to Lillian."

"Marty," I often said to him, "everything I know about the jewelry business I learned from you."

Marty would answer, "I was only a plater when we met.

I'm convinced that everything I know about the jewelry business, I learned from you."

The truth was, we grew up together. Together we mastered the intricacies of casting, stamping, buying filigree, enameling, soldering, and on time delivery.

When I began our own manufacturing company, the New Company, in Providence, Rhode Island, I financed the venture from our cash reserves. My personal savings, too, contributed at least 50 percent. A great early lesson for an entrepreneur: Risk your own money, trust your creative instincts, and find someone who can execute your vision.

The business, Lillian Vernon, was growing apace. Gold-filled and sterling rings for $1 brought in 30,000 orders. A little black compact—perfect for teenagers because it was shaped like a telephone dial—was so back-ordered that I spent weekend after weekend engraving these compacts. I was truly adept at the job. On a good Sunday, I could turn out eight hundred.

Soon, I needed to hire full-time help at home so I could work full time. Those were hectic times. I'd call on customers and cover trade fairs. I would set out on Monday morning, fly to Chicago, move on to Peoria, Evanston, and Oshkosh, take in Colorado Springs and Dallas, and end up in Los Angeles. In each city, I spent hours visiting factories and walking up and down trade-fair aisles. On Friday night, I'd fly home on the red-eye to arrive in New York at 6 A.M. Saturday—just in time to spend the weekend with my family. I loved those trips. Finding new merchandise was a refreshing and exhilarating experience. And the sale of something I had designed was a real delight.

I concentrated on items that were the best quality for the price. I was determined not to shortchange my customers. In those days, mail order had a questionable reputation. Lots of the products sold through catalogs were shoddy, and dissatisfied customers couldn't get their money back. I tried to make sure my customers were never disappointed, but if they were,

THE CUSTOMER IS YOUR FRIEND

From the outset, as a mail-order business, you need to be developing your customer database. I started mine when I sold my first bag. Once you have built a customer base, you must nurture it with care and patience. If the product is going to be late, be sure to let the customer know as quickly as possible. A postcard is the best way to do this. Include a definite future delivery date. There is now a federal law that mandates either thirty-day shipment or a postcard apprising customers of late delivery. Long before the law, my company followed this policy.

Chances are, you'll often find yourself on the telephone answering customer queries. Answer them fully, patiently, and honestly.

If a customer returns an item, refund the money as quickly as you can. Some mail-order houses refuse to accept returns beyond a certain deadline that ranges anywhere from thirty days to one year. Lillian Vernon accepts returns of even monogrammed items. That should tell you how important I believe it is to have a liberal return policy: it sustains customer goodwill. And if a customer calls to say that he or she has not received an order we know was shipped out, we simply replace the lost item, no questions asked. Tell your customers when you have made a mistake, and offer them a rebate—or even send them a future discount as compensation.

Always remember that without customers, you have no business: repeat customers are the firm foundation of any company.

I returned their money, and there was never a time limit on that promise. We have always refunded, in cash or in credit, always without hesitation. Here's an example we all talk about: Recently, a customer who was packing up her house to move found an unopened box of Old Foley stoneware from England. She'd ordered it twenty years earlier and now had no use for it. When she returned it to us, it took me a little while to dig through old catalogs for the price, $79.98, but we sent her a refund.

A Big Hit

What a heady time it was!

We expanded even further and opened a wholesale division. That came about because an established Atlantic City–based mail-order house, Spencer Gifts, inquired about the name of our jewelry manufacturer. Of course, the company at that time was my company. Before we quite realized it, we were manufacturing for Spencer Gifts. Spencer advertised our products in its own catalogs and sold them. We had taken on order fulfillment as well as manufacturing for other mail-order companies. By the end of that year, we had similar deals with at least four other mail-order companies.

By 1958, seven years after that first ad, the company was pulling in $500,000 in sales. I just started to think big—really BIG. There seemed to be no end to our potential growth. We had expanded our product line to include trimmed gloves and sweater guards to hold a sweater on the shoulders fashionably—monogrammed, the fashion look of today. My father still supplied our leather products. We manufactured the jewelry ourselves. And the rest of the products—items I had spotted at trade fairs—came from all over the United States.

ADVERTISING

Isn't it an exciting moment when you decide you're ready to place your first ad? But wait. Before you act, you should do some research. Your ad must be right in line with your product and the market you've targeted. Take some time to find out which magazine or newspaper will work hardest for you. If you're selling back-supporting car seats, for example, consider *Modern Maturity*, the magazine published by AARP, the American Association of Retired People.

Don't overlook the possibility of your local radio station as an advertising medium. The rates are likely to be low, and local stations will sometimes help prepare a tape—some stations may even be willing to cover your production costs.

Television is expensive and probably beyond the reach of your beginning budget. Even local television commercials add considerably to your advertising costs. Television can come later.

One of our biggest hits was the Hurry Door Knocker. In those days, most homes had only one bathroom, and our brass knocker was great for sending the message to slowpokes. The item did so well, we were able to buy our first house. At Sam's suggestion, we called it The House the Hurry Knocker Built. And, of course, we installed those door knockers—even though we had two baths. We had intended to buy a $25,000 house, but my business optimism was so great that we bought one for $35,000. It was an eight-room ranch in Mount Vernon—an easy drive to our office. I thought it was a palace. We had worked hard for it, and it made both Sam and me very happy and proud. It also gave me a sense of belonging and stability.

Not since I had left Germany had I lived in a house that was my own.

By 1960, our company had expanded so much that we needed more space. We were no longer working in Sam's old store but in a loft above a bar and grill on one of Mount Vernon's main avenues. But even that was becoming too crowded. Boxes were piled to the ceiling. Shippers worked at makeshift tables. Our filing system was getting out of hand. So we moved to bigger quarters in New Rochelle, still only minutes away from the house and our two children.

My Golden Gut

As the business continued to grow in the 1960s, so did my job of finding and choosing merchandise for our customers. Luckily, I never felt overwhelmed. I loved the responsibility and the fun. How did I know what would sell? I drew mostly on my own tastes or needs. Many of our customers were women like me, busy homemakers.

Shopping has intrigued me since childhood. I was lucky enough to be born with a natural eye—an intangible and innate talent. Perhaps it's like other arts. You can teach anyone a few simple dance steps, but you can't turn a klutz into Ginger Rogers. You can't turn a tone-deaf singer with a wobbly voice into Beverly Sills. And you can't make a first-class merchandiser out of someone who doesn't love to shop and doesn't have an eye. I like to think I was born with a golden gut when it comes to choosing what I sell. Something happens to me when I spot a hot product. I feel it in the pit of my stomach. I know.

When I chose the bookmark and the Hurry Door Knocker, I had no doubts that they were winners. And I've had similar successes in later years. Lillian Vernon has sold millions of crocheted snowflakes, which I discovered in the Philippines. Our first personalized brass Christmas ornaments—we called them commemoratives—were an instant hit. There was an angel in a star and a trumpeter in a circlet, and the customer could have them engraved with any name. We sold more than 100,000 that year, and we have offered Christmas commemoratives ever since. Sales totaled over ten million units.

Right from the start, I gave people what they wanted at a price they could afford. I concentrated on merchandise that would make their lives easier and a bit happier. Practical considerations always guided my shopping. The pace of my own life tipped me off. A time-saver was a lifesaver. This has become truer over the years. Americans will buy anything that shaves minutes off an hour. History has served me well. I came along just as women were entering the workforce in large numbers. They were grateful for the convenience of mail-order shopping and for the time my products saved them.

Apart from the pleasure and challenge of shopping, I have also always loved selecting presents. When you set out to buy gifts for people, you must keep images of them in your mind. You have to envision them in three dimensions and living color as you leaf through a catalog or peruse the aisles. And you have to factor in the element of surprise. I don't buy things for people that they will buy for themselves. I try to be imaginative and find something a little offbeat— useful, perhaps, but still unusual. For a friend who loves fruit, I once bought a handsome bowl decorated with a variety of fruits with their Latin and English names written below. A man I knew, who prided himself on his appearance and always carried an expensive leather briefcase, suddenly had to wear glasses. He carried them around in a cheap plastic case that just didn't fit with his man-about-town image. I bought him a leather case with his initials. You should look for presents that are in harmony with the recipients' personalities, not your own.

On the Lookout

If you want to be a first-class merchandiser, you must experience every part of life. Only then can you go out and buy what somebody else may want. I've heard people say, "Oh, the things I like wouldn't have mass appeal." I consider that attitude elitist: those people send a clear message that they consider their taste above that of other people. I do not feel that way. I'm using what I sell. Decorating my home with these products. I wear and I give gifts from my catalogs. I've never condescended to my customers, and I hope they know that.

A good merchandiser also keeps an eye open for social trends. I often feel like a social scientist, keeping an eye out

---

YOUR MARKET

Once you have hit on an idea, research your market. Find similar products and examine them carefully. This background work is another investment that will pay for itself. Ask yourself whether your idea and the way you execute it is better than what's already out there. The answer must be an unequivocal yes. Otherwise you won't be competitive. Do other products work as well as they should? As an example, you suffer from a bad back and sitting in a car is particularly uncomfortable. To ease your pain, you design an orthopedic seat cushion that really makes a difference. When your neighbor admires your custom-made seat, you have one made for her, too. Why not capitalize on the huge market of back-pain sufferers? Now is the time to buy and test similar products. If none of them measures up to yours, you will be set to take the plunge.

---

for changing attitudes, tastes, and needs. I noticed at one point that jug wines were becoming very popular. I noted that people stored them in their refrigerators, where they take up a lot of room. We designed a square wine decanter that was thin enough to store in the refrigerator door. We priced it at $5.98, and the first time we put it into our Christmas catalog we sold 145,000. Recently, we reintroduced that item to the same enthusiastic reception.

PRICING YOUR PRODUCT

To come up with a viable price for your product you must figure your costs carefully and honestly. I use the word *honestly* because it's so dangerously easy to ignore certain details of costs. You must figure in overhead expenses: what percentage for telephone, office supplies, and insurance should you charge to each item? To this figure, add the specific costs of manufacturing, storage, advertising, and delivery.

After you've computed these costs, you need to determine a reasonable profit. Should profits be 30 percent? 50 percent? More? You certainly don't want to price yourself out of the market, but you must do as well as you can to continue to grow. Check your competitors' prices. You might go a little lower to have customers running to you.

You want to offer your products at a compelling price. Selling more of something at a lower price is often more profitable than less of it for a larger margin. You can also create extra value by encouraging your customers to purchase your product in sets; when a customer places an order for two rather than one item, you save by shipping one package rather than two. It works!

I learned to always be on the lookout for merchandise. I still keep a little notebook to jot down things that intrigue me. Always alert to items I think my customers might buy. Whether in a car, in a store, or on the street, I carefully observe the world around us, searching for the perfect item that will break all sales records. One day, our jewelry distributor told me that he represented a company that made can openers and frozen-food saws. Guess what appeared in our next catalog? The frozen-food saw wasn't an enormous hit, but we did sell about 5,000.

One day, walking through Bloomingdale's, I spotted two little girls carrying a corrugated box. They were looking for the Bloomingdale's buyer. They told me they had candles they had made at home, which they hoped to sell to the store as Christmas items.

I explained that I was a buyer, and asked to see their products.

I peeked into a box full of cupcake-shaped candles in various colors. They were adorable—perfect merchandise for us. I ordered thousands of them, in all the colors. I was a little concerned that such young girls—they were sisters, those junior entrepreneurs, and couldn't have been more than twelve and fourteen years old—wouldn't be able to deliver. When I got back to the office, I called the telephone number the girls had given me and talked to their mother. She explained that the children had been told that they must earn money for their college tuition. And yes, she said, the kids would deliver. With that assurance, we went ahead and put the candles into our Christmas catalog. When I talked to their mother again, she confessed that the family's kitchen had been unusable for weeks and that they had barely been able to eat a meal at home—even on Thanksgiving. Their daughters' venture probably cost the parents ten times what the girls earned, but it taught these children a valuable lesson. We ended up ordering over 10,000 pieces, and they were a huge success—such a huge success, that other companies started to copy them, and in time we had to move on. I think of Abigail and Esther Resnick often and wish more parents would do what theirs did to encourage and educate their children.

In my years as a merchandiser, I have tried to unearth the unique. For four decades, I scoured merchandise fairs in this country, gradually extending my range from New York to Chicago to California. I never wanted to miss any promising items, so I spent three or four days at each show, walking the aisles, examining all the vendors' offerings, comparing one piece of merchandise with another. All the while, I weighed prices against possible sales and profits per item. In later years, as the company grew, that quest has taken me around the world many times. I'm a traveler and that's one of the best parts of my job. I wouldn't like my job if I couldn't travel.

Early on, I developed the habit of taking notes on merchandise. If I saw a vase that appealed to me, I'd jot down a description of it and try to find the manufacturer or have a designer make copies for my catalog. I was always with a pad and pen. Even with my children, I sat and scribbled. Someone once asked me why I was so obsessed with lists and notes.

"Once I write something down," I answered, "I don't have to worry about remembering it. That saves mental energy, and I can concentrate on something else." My staff became used to receiving my scrawled memos and nick-named them "Lilly's Notes." I love writing so much—ad copy, notes, stories, headlines—my friends and family question whether I have ink in my veins.

Flare-ups

By the early 1960s, Lillian Vernon had turned a major corner. We had diversified, started making our own line of products, opened a wholesale business, moved to a much larger building, and started to publish a catalog. All of that brought out the best in me and—when the office got really hectic—the worst.

You could make a chart of a successful entrepreneur's business showing two lines: one representing success and another tracing emotional outbursts. Both rise parallel to each other, but once in a while they intersect. Inevitably, success leads to pressure, and, sooner or later that pressure is going to lead to an explosion. I felt pressured because I thought so much was expected of me, and I never quite

GROWTH

Growth brings opportunities and complications. The opportunities for making money—maybe a lot of it—are there, but before that can happen, you may find yourself coping with unexpected problems. All your expenses will take an enormous leap. Don't forget that increasing your sales also means that you must invest more in product, warehousing, and fulfillment. You have to hire more employees, and most likely you'll need to move to larger quarters. You will have to concentrate on finding just the right kinds of employees for your business. While recruiting is time-consuming, it is worth the investment.

If you have been able to manage without outside financing, you may need it now. You will have to reconsider your own role in the company. When my company grew at a phenomenal rate in the 1980s, I suddenly had to change my way of doing business. It was hard. I had to hand over the reins of management to others and to let the people I had hired make decisions that had previously been mine.

understood that other people neither reacted as quickly as I did nor set their priorities exactly in line with mine. People never seemed to get things done as quickly. When the pressure got too much, off I would go, acting like a tormented and sad soul.

After I had cooled down from one of my ugly displays of bad manners, the person I berated most harshly was myself. I would spend days in anguish at my rude and unnecessary behavior.

I couldn't always keep a rein on my emotions. Mistakes—an employee's or my own—could set off a burst of temper.

I maintain that the occasional honest outburst isn't a bad way to manage. Consultants tell me that outbursts are typical of classic entrepreneurs. Risk brings entrepreneurs close to their emotional edge, and they find themselves beset with anxieties. An eruption, caused by even the smallest thing going wrong, is a natural release. Furthermore, because entrepreneurs are their own bosses, they are not—like their employees—constrained by social conventions to bite their tongues. Employees, for the most part, know that blowing up at their boss is not a great way to get ahead. It was in character for me to be upset and angry when something went wrong. On the other hand, I know that consideration goes a long way. And I have never been one to harbor resentments or carry a grudge for more than a few minutes. I've tried to temper my anguish with praise and move quickly beyond mistakes.

Family Life

Despite those early years of hard work and long hours, Sam and I enjoyed ourselves—each other and our children. I didn't want to lead the nose-to-the-grindstone life my parents had endured during their many years of struggle after we left Germany. We both liked going to parties and throwing our own. We went out dancing or off to the theater. We enjoyed weekends with Fred and David at the zoo or the movies. We took them to children's parties and gave parties for them at home. We went on vacations to the Amish country in Pennsylvania and skiing in Vermont. Sam took the boys sailing and taught them to play tennis. Unfortunately, neither of the boys liked these athletic pursuits that their father enjoyed so much. It was a disappointment to him. Sam and I spent our free time at home with Fred and David. We played board games together. Monopoly was a favorite. I never went out during the week. I believed very strongly that since I worked all day, I wanted to be home with my children at night. After I had cooked dinner, and the children were asleep, I worked. I always had lists to check and orders to catch up on. You know a woman's work is never done.

Many people believe that successful entrepreneurs think, dream, and live their businesses. I also believe that time spent away from the business brings a fresh eye, broadens the horizon, and creates new contacts. I wish now that we had taken more vacations in the early years, but even then I never did focus on my business life to the exclusion of all else. Networking—keeping in touch with the outside world—is an excellent way to find out what is going on. It's basic to good business, and I wish I had done more at earlier stages of my career. I have learned more from talking to other people at parties than I ever did from trade papers or studying a balance sheet. Not so long ago, I was at a spa where I met a woman who offered to help me open the Mexican market. On a recent visit to Montreux, Switzerland, I ran into one of her friends. She recognized me and expressed her interest in helping us, and in time she did. It's a small connected world for us all.

Although we had fun at play, Sam and I frequently clashed at work. Where I was fearless, he was cautious. If I put in an order for 10,000 pieces, he would cut the order in half.

"If you want to gamble, go to Las Vegas," he grumbled more than once.

"Sam," I said, "you have to spend money to make money."

Ordering too few of an item meant we would need to reorder, and then the customer would have to wait. Even worse, the manufacturer might run out of materials and we would lose a sale, maybe even a customer. Repeat business is all-important in mail order. The customer comes back for more because she likes what she's bought. I knew the importance of customer service from the start. Sam didn't, and he never understood the heart of mail order. He was used to meeting his customers face-to-face in his family store. He never learned that in mail order—where you don't see your customers—the customer relationship is built on trust.

7

BREAKTHROUGH

Moving into the Big Time

—

An Irreplaceable Loss

—

The Catalog Is Born

—

Divorce

—

Moving into the Big Time

Vernon Specialties Company was born in 1951, on the day I sat down with my father to design my first monogrammed bags and belts. But I mark 1962 as the year in which the company came of age.

My father—my mentor for so many years—followed, for the first time, in *my* footsteps, beginning a mail-order business of his own in the 1950s. He gave it the name he had used for his other companies, Mercury Products, and his company sold, primarily, the personalized jewelry I manufactured. One of his few nonjewelry products was a personalized magnetic bobby-pin cup decorated with filigree that I manufactured. In those days, most women used bobby pins, and they were always slipping down the drain, falling on the floor, dropping behind the sink. The magnetized cup was a secure place to store them. It was pretty, feminine, and useful all at once—and it caught the eye of Revlon, the cosmetics giant.

On January 18, 1962, Revlon opened its first account with us. Although the bobby-pin cup had attracted Revlon's attention, the company purchased only my golden metal filigree and used it to decorate its own perfume bottles, soap dishes, candles, and candleholders. A big account? You bet! It was worth a couple of million dollars to Lillian Vernon. It's hard to describe how it felt. In those days, Revlon was the leader of the cosmetics industry. I was doing business with the best. In the eyes of the business world, the account bestowed legitimacy on my company and on me. Working with Revlon eventually led to orders for metal filigree from such companies as Max Factor, Elizabeth Arden, and Helena Rubinstein. The experience was really my second MBA. The executives of those companies, especially Revlon, taught me to apply what I had heard at my parents' dinner table.

Revlon drove hard bargains. Once, when the company wanted to renegotiate a price per unit, and I agreed to new figures, my decision really upset Sam.

"Lillian, your price is too low. A deal that tight leaves us no margin for error. One mistake could bankrupt us."

"Then we will make sure that we do everything exactly right," I answered.

Revlon was both a hard bargainer and notorious for returning shipments. Perhaps the latter was part of its well-known quality control. It wasn't unusual for the company to claim that our plating was too dark or too light or that some of the items arrived dented. We often found nothing amiss with the shipments they returned to us. Occasionally we found an item that had been damaged in shipping—a disappointment, but an inevitability when you ship millions of pieces.

During this time we were also making jewelry for Spencer Gifts, which introduced a special catalog for charms. The company's president gave me carte blanche to design and manufacture charms for that new catalog. It was a flattering and unprecedented offer. We produced a whole line of charms, from ballerinas to sports symbols, from baby charms to graduation memorabilia. They were attractive, original designs, and they sold very well for many years!

An Irreplaceable Loss

My father's death on January 11, 1962, darkened the triumph of winning the Revlon account. I mourned him, and left my children for a week to stay with my mother. Every day, almost every waking moment, his memory was before me, reminding me of all he had done to shape my life. When I went to Revlon's office to sign the contract, on January 18, I was still in mourning. At one point I excused myself and retreated to the ladies' room. Fighting back tears, I looked at myself in the mirror. I saw a self-assured, competent woman on the verge of her greatest accomplishment. I also saw an insecure girl, an outsider, still struggling for knowledge and experience. "I wish you were here with me," I said aloud, summoning up my father's image. He had guided my earliest ventures, encouraged and inspired me. Now he was gone. After my brother, Fred, was killed, my father never fully recovered, and I know that loss hastened his death at age sixty-three.

Despite his overwhelming sadness, he had been a loving, generous grandfather. He would take Fred and David for special treats all over New York. Perhaps they reminded him of the son he'd lost. My boys missed him terribly. I despaired that they would grow up without his love and his example. I wish he'd been with us all for many more years, just as I wish my children could have known their uncle and known the pleasures and love of a larger extended family.

The Catalog Is Born

In the 1960s another factor sent my business soaring. At first we had drawn all our orders with our magazine ads. When I started to include an unassuming four-page mini-catalog with each order, we had entered a new phase. The mini-catalog, illustrated with black-and-white photographs, promoted new products. I wrote the copy, and we used my hands and feet to model certain items. The response was so good that we turned those mini-catalogs into catalogs that we mailed directly to our customers, whether or not they had recently placed orders. And we also began advertising the catalogs themselves in a brand new advertising campaign.

YOUR CATALOG

Once you have a substantial customer base and an expanded product line, you will be ready to publish a catalog. Be realistic. A beginner's catalog can be very effective, even if it consists of only a couple of pages and offers no more than fifty items. If the response is good, then you can move on to a bigger and better publication. Printing and mailing costs are high today. You will also need an art director, a copywriter, and a photographer—in other words, a creative team.

A full-blown catalog should offer at least a hundred products, run to twenty-four pages, and have a mailing list of at least 200,000 customers. In my experience, no item should list for less than $5 or $10, but beyond that, offer products that cover a broad price range. You should aim for an average sale of $30 to $40. Do at least two, preferably four, mailings a year, and carry an inventory of 33 percent of the items you are selling, depending where you source. If your sources are abroad, more coverage is needed. If you can find wonderful things here in the United States, smaller up-front commitments are needed.

Before you launch your catalog, make sure that your delivery system functions smoothly. Competition in the mail-order business is fierce, and customers expect their orders to arrive on time. You should investigate a fulfillment house, a company that will do the back end of your business at a cost.

I have found that a well-designed catalog can increase sales. We often feature a special item to attract attention, and we use background colors to enhance the appearance of all our items. We leave enough room for good, explanatory copy. And we spend a lot of time on our covers, front and back. If a new customer gets one of our catalogs and doesn't find the covers appealing, she may never bother to look at the merchandise inside. My best advice is to do it well right up front so you can grow your business. Had my first ad not been so wildly successful, I would probably be the mother of ten children and a hardworking volunteer. The choice is yours.

For a nickel apiece, we printed our first catalog—thirty-two black-and-white pages that featured 175 items, most of them priced between $1.00 and $2.98—and mailed it to 125,000 people.

Orders poured into my tiny office, and I had to hire extra part-time people, mostly mothers or homemakers who could work only during school hours. Crammed together, we all opened envelopes, sorted orders, kept track of money, monogrammed everything, and addressed and mailed out packages. We were so crowded that at meetings people had to perch on file cabinets. It was mayhem, but we all loved it. Working so closely together, we developed an exhilarating team spirit—almost a sense of family. In those early days, I often drove employees home when we worked late. I knew about their families. In later years, when the business expanded and our staff had grown into the hundreds, I couldn't keep up with everyone in the same way. Even so, I've done my best to learn people's names and pay attention to important moments in their lives. People never forget such small acts of kindness. Some of those employees are still with us today.

Our office grew so crowded that we had to move once again. This time we acquired a plant in New Rochelle that measured 5,000 square feet. It was a big step up from our previous space. We had been there only a couple of months when, out of the blue, disaster—only inches from tragedy—struck. On the last Friday in June (we were closing early for the July Fourth weekend), out of nowhere a massive cement mixer came crashing through the walls of the building and into the warehouse. One of our employees, Madeline Manto, was still busy packing when she heard the noise, saw the truck coming toward her, and froze in panic. Sam threw out his arms and shouted, "Run! Run to me!" Thank God his words cut through her fear and she acted. The damage to our space, though, took months to repair. The truck made a huge hole in the roof, and rain poured in, soaking merchandise, shipments, and all our records. It was, for the Lillian Vernon Corporation, a heart-rending and financial setback we could not afford. We became entangled in claims and counter-claims. The trucking company asserted that the nearby filling station—where the truck was gassing up when it went out of control—was at fault. The owner of the station claimed that the truck was overloaded and blamed the trucking company. Finally, both tried to fault the contractor of our build-ing, claiming he had done a sloppy construction job. Years later, we collected about $5,000—approximately twenty times less than we had lost.

When we moved into our New Rochelle quarters, we had substantial cash flow, so we were able to expand without borrowing. Years earlier, when I desperately needed extra space, the landlord had called for a security deposit—cash I did not have. I did, however, have some World War II bonds, which I had been given in the early 1940s, a time when everyone bought bonds. I kept them in my safety-deposit box and used them as collateral whenever I was in urgent need of cash. In those early days, I beat quite a path between the bank vault and the loan department. My well-traveled bonds kept the company going for years: to my bankers the assets of the Lillian Vernon Corporation were considered risky collateral. To begin with, I was a woman, and financial people viewed—and often still view—women in business as intrinsically poor risks. What's more, few bankers in those days really understood the mail-order business: no machin-

---

INSURANCE

A good insurance broker can be your best friend when you're starting a business. At a minimum, a competent broker will most likely advise you to buy a product-liability policy to protect you against a lawsuit claiming injury from one of your products. You should also consider fire and theft policies to cover damage to your inventory. If you use your car for your business, you will have to increase your personal automobile coverage. Insurance premiums can be high. To find the most favorable rates, check to see whether you can join a professional or industry association that offers group benefits. Remember, your corporate structure will affect your insurance requirements.

---

ery, no manufacturing. In their eyes, there was no collateral. My absolutely irreplaceable and invaluable list of customers was considered intangible, and in the eyes of the bankers, didn't qualify for a loan.

Even today, women who want to start businesses are reticent about dealing with banks. When I talk to women's groups about the Lillian Vernon Corporation, the most frequently asked questions concern banks. Women want to know how to approach a bank for a loan. What kind of collateral do banks accept? Did I have a special banker when I began? Some women even ask me what they should wear when they go to a bank meeting.

When my children were young, I discovered that the prejudice against working women wasn't limited to banks. Hardly a week went by without a phone call from a neighbor telling me, sweetly, that she had heard my children crying after I left them with the housekeeper. I knew and trusted the woman I had hired to look after Fred and

David, and I believed that resentment and jealousy fueled those calls. The housekeeper may have cleaned and done the laundry, but I took care of my family: I called the plumber or electrician, got the slipcovers dry-cleaned, and attended to the other details of running a home. And I raised my children with love and attention.

Divorce

It was on a rainy day in March 1968 that I began to have serious doubts about my marriage. I had told Sam that I wanted to spend $75,000 for a single month of magazine advertising. He looked at me as if we didn't belong to the same species. Then it hit me: perhaps we didn't. The entrepreneurial spirit was not in Sam. My drive and determination disturbed him. It was as if we lived in parallel universes. It dawned on me gradually that it was only a matter of time before we would end our private life together.

Sam's greatest satisfaction came from playing tennis and sailing. Those activities didn't appeal to me. We both loved to read, and we both enjoyed the theater, but I also liked to go out on the town, experiment with new restaurants, explore places I'd never visited, and learn about other cultures. I got a kick out of decorating our home. Much of what gave me pleasure left Sam cold. I was more emotionally involved in the business than he was. He worked very hard, but he came in at 9 A.M. and left at 5 P.M., and he couldn't understand why I took work home in the evenings. But it was not the business that drove us apart. It was our dissimilar temperaments. While we shared a zest for living, over time the paths we traveled had diverged.

Divorce is always a serious business, and in those days it was a good deal less common than it is today. Faced with crucial life decisions, I went into therapy. I'll never forget my relief when I realized that there was someone—not a relative, not a friend, but a compassionate professional—who could help me.

I spent many hours working through my anxiety, guilt, and fear. I worried about my mother's reaction to my split from Sam. No one in my family had ever divorced. Fortunately, she took it more calmly than I had expected. Perhaps she understood more than I had given her credit for.

I have a friend who asserts that she knew within a week of her wedding that her marriage was a mistake, but it took her fourteen years to get up the courage to leave. I completely understand: it's a slow, agonizing journey from realization to action.

Twenty years after our wedding, I told Sam it wasn't going to work.

The dinner plates were in the dishwasher, and the boys were upstairs doing their homework. It would be easier for both of us if I spoke without hesitation.

"Sam," I said. He looked up at me inquisitively, exactly as I'd seen him do thousands of times in the past. I gathered my strength. "I want a divorce."

He was shocked into silence. A look of pain and sadness passed over his face. He knew there were problems as well as I did; he just never thought I would take this final step. Finally, he said, "I've got to give you credit, Lillian. You've got real guts, you always have."

With the decision made, it was easiest for us to act quickly. I flew to Mexico to get a divorce. Sam didn't try to stop me, but gave me one warning: "When you need me, I may be remarried." He issued it without malice, and even now I'm grateful to Sam for his generous spirit, his kindness to me, all the love he showered on our children, and his support with the business.

Sure, there were bad moments. How could life be otherwise? A few months later, my son David became a bar mitzvah. Sam and I sat at separate tables, which hurt David. I tried to explain to him why the marriage didn't work, that it was a matter of different goals and temperaments and had nothing to do with him or Fred. Did he understand? Does a child ever understand when parents separate? I can't be sure. What I do know is that David handled the situation with grace and maturity. In his new suit, reading from the Torah in a recently deepened voice, I saw that he really was coming of age.

And I was coming of age, too. With my father gone and my marriage over, I was truly my own woman, ready to make a new life.

For a year, Sam and I continued to work together, but it was difficult, and finally we made a settlement. Sam assumed the wholesale end of the company—he'd always enjoyed that part—and I kept the mail-order business, at that time the company's stepchild. The wholesale business was worth about $5 million in sales, mail order less than a million. A stipulation in the agreement said that I could not sell wholesale for three years. I wanted the little business because mail order was my first and abiding love. The catalog was my baby—and a thriving baby ready to move ahead.

As a single mother and businesswoman, my juggling act became more difficult. Not long ago, I read an interview with a businesswoman. When asked what she most needed, she responded: a wife. Exactly!

In one area, my struggles gave me an advantage: I had a first-hand understanding of the needs of the women who worked for me. Flexible hours were and are the answer. I once met a businessman who told me that he wanted to hire a woman for a big job. She would take it only if she could have every Thursday afternoon off to watch her daughter play on her school basketball team. Being a wise man, he accepted her conditions, and he never regretted it. We ran some pretty crazy schedules, too. Some people came to work at 8 or 9 A.M. and stayed until noon. Others worked until 3 P.M., when they left to pick up their young children from school. Others came in to pick up work—typing, for instance—that they would do at home.

Like all mail-order businesses, we have to rely on a large seasonal staff, especially at Christmas. Our current warehouse, built in 1988, in Virginia Beach, hires some 4,000 seasonal employees. Many of those people return to us year after year. That's remarkable in the mail-order business and an indication that they like working for Lillian Vernon.

We offered employees tuition reimbursement and four-month pregnancy leaves. I instituted those policies because I felt strongly that treating people decently and humanely was the only way to run a good, solid business.

We have always had parties—both planned and impromptu. For all our employees, we've had elegant events at fashionable New York hotels and casual affairs such as our day-long annual picnics. At Christmas, we have a gala. I love planning, organizing, and hosting parties. We give each of our five- and ten-year employees a gift from Tiffany's. I often invite coworkers to Sunday brunch. And birthdays! We make quite a fuss about birthdays, celebrating them with cake and gifts. It's one of the ways we try to maintain a family atmosphere in this ever-expanding company.

8

A TWENTY-YEAR OVERNIGHT SUCCESS

Lillian Vernon's Catalog

—

Keep It Simple

—

Finding Our Customers

—

Keeping the Customer Happy

—

Gifts for Our Customers

—

In 1970 the Lillian Vernon Corporation broke the $1 million sales barrier.

It should have come as no surprise, but it did. I called it my twenty-year overnight success: twenty years of business stops and starts.

The $1 million had more than symbolic value. This was back when a million was a million. In the 1980s, there was a joke about a painting that went for $10 million at an auction. One person says, "But that painting isn't worth $10 million." The other person answers, "The $10 million isn't worth $10 million." I ended that memorable decade on quite a high.

Throughout the 1960s, as the company grew step by step, I was able to hone my skills. I had gone from being an apprentice to being a leader in my industry. At the same time, in my personal life, I had gone through the trauma of a divorce. And my sons, growing up through difficult teenage years and through a divorce, needed a lot of care and attention.

I look back on 1970 now and realize that it marked a major transition in my business career and my personal life. For twenty years I had built my business, but it was still in some ways a mom-and-pop operation—after the divorce, a mom-alone operation. In that year, I stood on the threshold of the big time. The skills, the knowledge, and the experience I had gained over two decades of hard work and intense commitment were in place, and I was ready to move forward.

The next ten years were successful beyond my most extravagant expectations. In both 1973 and 1974, our sales doubled. In 1976, we had revenues of $6 million. By 1982, the company's revenues had risen to more than $60 million.

I was already an experienced and well-trained practitioner

GROW WITH CAUTION

It is tempting for a new entrepreneur to speed ahead as quickly as possible. My advice is to research and test. I began with only two leather products. I became my own teacher. Anyone starting up a mail-order company is wise to follow a careful route. Stick to one or two products, and don't add more until you have established your market. Then add as quickly as possible. You have your accountant to help you. You will learn how to merchandise, how to keep exact records, and how to cope with fulfillment so that when you grow you will have a fingertip feeling for the mechanics of running your company. Above all, you will accumulate cash, which can keep your company afloat when you begin to expand.

---

of the art of mail order. I understood merchandising, I had learned how to put together a catalog, and I knew the importance of customer relationships. The ins and outs and the dos and don'ts of the mail-order business were second nature to me. That didn't mean that I wouldn't face serious challenges in the following decades.

Success inevitably brought change to the company. There were areas of the business where my knowledge of mail order was no help: finance, administration, and the management of our customer lists grew increasingly complex—really beyond my knowledge and training. In the year of that momentous $1 million achievement, I saw that I would have to reorganize the Lillian Vernon Corporation. At first I wasn't quite sure of myself, but I knew I had to approach growth seriously. I was secure as a businesswoman, ready to sail ahead and meet whatever problems and challenges awaited me.

Despite the inevitable changes, my priorities remained the same. I gave time and attention to finding merchandise—over the next ten years I broadened my search to Europe and Asia, to publishing more catalogs, and to nurturing my customers and employees.

I continued to work as hard as ever. My day started early, with breakfast for the boys. They attended Hackley Day School in nearby Tarrytown, so we all left the house together. I seldom arrived at the office later than 8 A.M. Once there, I poured a cup of coffee and walked around greeting everyone. Next, I checked the data on sales trends—especially the sales statistics of items featured on the back and front covers of the current catalog. I reviewed the number of free gifts we sent: those numbers are good indicators of overall sales. I spent the rest of the day in meetings with the merchandising department, the fulfillment staff, our finance group, and anyone who had problems of any kind—and someone always did. Every day I made about one hundred decisions—large and small.

Lillian Vernon's Catalog

My early experience convinced me that finding the right catalog merchandise is the key to all mail-order businesses. If your merchandise meets the needs of the market, customers will follow. How you present your merchandise—the design and production of your catalog—also has a lot to do with how well customers receive it.

The most successful catalogs are those with distinctive personalities. The image is sharpest when the catalog bears the stamp of a single person's spirit and taste. In the case of Lillian Vernon, that stamp was my own. By going out to cover trade shows, work with suppliers, search new sources of merchandise, and find companies to manufacture the merchandise I needed, I established early on the special character of the Lillian Vernon catalog. I could have sat at my desk and sent others to search for me. I would have weeded through their selections, but I don't believe the results would have been the same. In time, the distinctive character of my catalog would have dimmed and, finally, faded away altogether.

Since we sent our very first catalog in 1960, I have given time and thought to establishing the identity of the Lillian Vernon catalog. I saw it as the company's standard-bearer. After all, it was through those pages that I communicated with my customers, and they judged my company by its catalog. I wanted to send them a message they could respond to; I made sure my catalog had a distinctive personality, that our merchandise would give the catalog its uniqueness. By 1974, the catalog had expanded to ninety-six pages, and most of it was in color.

Somehow, over the years, those of us who have worked on the catalog have internalized its personality. When one of my people comes to me and says that some item or other is not Lillian Vernon, I listen carefully. While we often have disagreements on this or that point, we always agree that everyone's overall vision must be in sync. We want our merchandise to be original, affordable, attractive, useful, and fun. We often include items that will make our customers smile: In an early black-and-white catalog, I featured place mats designed to be used under the bowl of a pampered pet. On the back cover of a 1995 catalog, we offered a three-foot stuffed figure of a Pilgrim, holding a personalized apple basket, for our customers to hang on their front doors, ready to greet guests.

Keep It Simple

Gradually, in the 1950s and 1960s, the nature of the mail-order business changed. Specialization was becoming increasingly important. The original bible of the mail-order business was the Montgomery Ward catalog, followed close-ly by the Sears, Roebuck catalog. With good reason, both were known in the trade as The Big Books. They were huge and offered everything from stoves to dungarees. The Big Books aimed largely at the rural market, which pretty well melted away after World War II. The suburban market replaced that rural market, and for suburban consumers, I realized you have to specialize.

My experience taught me that "Keep it simple" is a good motto for any mail-order business. During the early years focusing on specific merchandise gave my catalog the char-acter I wanted it to have, and that also increased sales and profits. I have kept to that policy ever since. I have never sold clothes or shoes. We did try to sell specialty foods, but were not successful. We tried too early, before the gourmet craze hit America. We cannot be all things to all people: there are just too many products to sell and too many people to sell them to.

To know your market, you must know your customer. The most successful catalogs today are those that cater—and I do mean *cater*—to their own special slice of our large national market. Their merchandise is highly selective. If you're going camping, you will buy from L. L. Bean or a sim-ilar outdoor catalog. But you don't expect to find your daughter's graduation dress in the pages of a Williams Sonoma kitchen catalog. There are now catalogs that special-ize in everything: linens, kitchenware, shoes, health products, even lingerie and "adult toys."

Our catalog has always had the feel of an old-fashioned general store: we feature a diversified line of products. We keyed into a yearning for a more personal time, a time when simple values and an upbeat outlook were the norm for American families. We identified a desire for affordable, use-ful, and basic merchandise and filled the need.

Throughout the history of the Lillian Vernon catalog we have retained the same category of merchandise and look.

We still try to satisfy that yearning. And, like a well-stocked general store, we're proud of our variety. We sell seasonal merchandise: Easter windsocks, leprechauns, Battenberg Christmas angels, and twinkling pearl Christmas lights. In addition, we offer practical items such as pedometers and lint removers. There are personal items such as leather bags and a triple magnifying glass for putting on contact lenses and makeup, as well as fun things like bricks to build castles in the sky, and dress-up trunks.

We aim to capture the imagination of Americans—women, for the most part—in their forties, employed outside the home. Our sales volume represents 19.4 million people who share my love of shopping. I cherish the responsibility of finding what is needed to fill those catalog pages with enticing products.

When on a merchandising trip, examining tens of thousands of products, I always keep a clear image of my customer in mind. She is a real person. She wants to save time, solve a problem, and brighten her life. I know her tastes, her likes, and her dislikes. That doesn't mean I don't misjudge her. From time to time, those of us who work on the catalog have been surprised when she completely ignores an item we thought she would love. There was the sleeping bag in the shape of a cat: few takers. A rolling pin you could fill with ice to make rolling out pastry easier: she didn't go for that either.

What does the customer need or want? Today we use very sophisticated technology to keep up with changing tastes and demographics. But in the early days, all we did was hope for the best. Since the 1970s, we've used focus groups to help gauge customer reaction to our merchandise. We hire professionals to set up those groups. We invite homemakers who work outside the home: they comprise some 65 percent of our customer base. We sit behind a one-way mirror, seeing but unseen. The group leader may show the women a Lillian Vernon catalog cover or an inside page. The women

MERCHANDISING

Of all activities in the mail-order business, none is more creative than merchandising. It's the part of my business I have loved the most. Your business will stand or fall on the quality of the products you offer. Here is where a natural eye and the ability to spot salable items are paramount. Visit trade fairs and be prepared to spend time and effort finding exactly what you need. I read magazines from all over the world to find the best products. Investing your energies in hunting for the right merchandise will repay you. There will be times when your customers reject a product you considered a real winner. Don't fall so much in love with your selection that you think your customer a fool. As long as most of what you sell draws a profitable response, don't get discouraged. Above all, trust your gut reactions. Don't let people talk you out of a product if your instincts tell you that it will sell.

discuss it, analyze it, and generally react to the layout and the products. For us, the feedback from these sessions is invaluable. The women's reactions guide our merchandise selections and give us an idea of how our customers will respond to our catalogs in general.

The meteoric rise of the specialty mail-order businesses, which began in the 1960s and then moved into two decades of runaway expansion, meant that competition in the field grew tougher. In 1951, when I entered the business, there were only about fifty such catalogs. Today, that number has grown to over 10,000. The steady increase in the number of working women, the introduction of credit cards in the mid–1960s, and the proliferation of 800 numbers are all factors that contributed to the growing popularity of mail order. To survive amid the competition, you had to know where you were heading. Suddenly, there were a lot of companies vying for the attention and dollars of the consumer. Our selection of merchandise and the way we presented it in the catalog became more critical. At the same time, production costs—paper, printing, and postage—were rising steadily. It became more important than ever that each catalog be on target. My first catalog cost five cents to mail. By the 1970s, the cost had increased six or seven times. Although I was proud of reaching the $1 million mark in 1970, I knew I would have to work long and hard for the Lillian Vernon Corporation to remain in a leadership position.

Over the years, people often told me that I ran the business by the seat of my pants. If it were only true that I ran my business purely by instinct, how much easier my life would have been. While it's true that instinct played a part, I tempered my natural talents with hard work, training, and experience. Instinct will get you started, but it won't sustain you: after all, your competitors have instincts, too. So you have to augment your natural gifts with good strategic planning and day-to-day immersion in the nitty-gritty of your enterprise. Without the proper amount of each ingredient, you won't capture the winning edge. In a business like ours, time-consuming—and often wearisome—attention to detail is crucial.

In the early days of the 1960s, when I never had enough time at home or at the office, I learned to understand the importance of attending to the small details. I used to take day trips to Providence to make sure the manufacturer was making my one simple little item exactly the way I wanted it. I read every word of the catalog before we mailed it. I still do. I knew where our inventory stood, how employees were handling orders, and a host of other details. Details are the foundation of any enterprise. After all, you don't start to build a house by putting on its roof.

Finding Our Customers

The best merchandise in the world, displayed in the handsomest catalog, won't get you anywhere unless you find people who want to buy it. The search for customers is one of the biggest—and most essential—undertakings of the mail-order business. I began with small ads, which increased in size and number as the business grew. For years, we counted on advertising to bring us customers. We concentrated our ads in established women's and fashion magazines. When we began to publish a catalog, that added to our customer base.

To find and keep customers, we had to pinpoint our most profitable areas. After we installed our first computer, we pored over our printouts to determine what customers had bought and what they had not wanted. We sold a tongue-in-cheek witch's kit, but customers rejected it as the work of the devil. They also rejected a plaque that we thought was cute: it said, "Marriage is a mutual misunderstanding." We couldn't sell our customers greeting cards for divorcées. On the other hand, we continue to be enormously successful with our commemorative line of Christmas ornaments.

The angel in a star and the trumpeter in a circle Christmas ornaments were such successes that I wanted to add new designs right away, but the tools were too expensive in those early days. They would have set us back $5,000. But by 1970, we were able to add other ornaments: a bell with a church scene and carolers. In our 1972 catalog we sold a sensational 250,000 pieces. We now called this line Lilly's Twinkles, and we registered the name. Eventually we developed 250 designs, and registered and copyrighted each one. We designed a silhouette of a boy and of a girl, we sold grandmother and grandfather Twinkles, and even a teacher Twinkle—one of our all time best-sellers. We even did a line of Norman Rockwell designs and a group called the Moppets. Because of the huge success of Twinkles ornaments, we learned to be careful and protective of our merchandise. Other businesses were going to the Far East to copy our designs. Our copyrights protected our products. Even so, Twinkles' success led us to court.

A manufacturer of sterling silver, whose specialty was selling copies of other people's merchandise, sued in 1987. He maintained that the Lillian Vernon Corporation was in violation of the Sherman Anti-Trust Act. I still can't understand why he did it. His company was in the multimillion-dollar bracket, and our Lilikins did only $2 million a year—a lot for us but a trifle for him. We appeared before Judge Robert Carter in New York City. Our opponent claimed that the stamping on the back of each ornament was not clear enough to register the copyright. We were able to prove to the judge that it was, and we won.

The telephone has always been an invaluable link with my customers. The opportunity to chat and answer their queries has its own rewards. In the early years, I often answered the phone myself: there was nobody else to do it. As we expanded, that became a telemarketer's job, but when I worked late, and everybody else had gone home, I was the one to answer. Customers called to discuss their orders, to ask questions about particular items, and to tell me how much they liked or disliked my catalog. No matter how complete we make our catalog descriptions, customers will always have questions. "Is 'one hundred-percent cotton' long- or short-staple cotton?" "Is 'cerise' more purple or red?" "Is this toy appropriate for an infant?" We answer all queries patiently. I have always known that eventually I could convert those telephone callers into customers.

Customer trust makes or breaks you. Customers are too smart to be fooled by fancy photography and overblown copy. Better to surprise a customer pleasantly than fail to meet expectations.

There are times—not often—when customers have been unhappy buying from a mail-order catalog. The Direct Marketing Association tries to protect our industry, largely by refusing to rent lists—to or from any company with a bad reputation. You, the customer, can avoid getting burned if you follow certain rules: Be careful when you buy from a catalog that lists only a post office box address. Keep a record of what you have ordered and when. Hold onto the catalog so that you can call if your order is not fulfilled or sent promptly. Every order has an order number, so if you order by phone, be sure to get that number. And remember that catalogs are safer than ads, because someone can run an ad just once. Some magazines won't run ads that elicit more than three complaints in one month. Catalogs are usually the product of reputable companies that have been in the business for years.

Keeping the Customer Happy

I have this rule of thumb: every unhappy customer will tell ten others about a bad experience, whereas happy customers may tell three.

We bend over backward to make sure that our customers aren't disappointed in Lillian Vernon. We are one of a handful of companies that gives refunds even on monogrammed items. If we—or other mail-order businesses—disappoint a customer, that customer will sour on *all* mail orders. We are in this together. If a customer calls us to complain of a non-delivery, we track it down and replace it, no questions asked. One reason we get an enormous amount of repeat business is our well earned reputation for honesty and reliability.

Our company handles numerous calls—100,000 weekly. I am always happy when I get a thank-you note: "We are thrilled with each item," writes one lady; another mentions she "particularly likes the imports from Italy"; a third writes she is "amazed at the variety and excellence of the products. I can usually find an item on every page that I would like to own." One year we put vinyl-covered paper clips, which did not rust, into the catalog. What pleased all of us most was a letter from a teacher of handicapped children, telling us that his students loved playing with the clips. When you have exhausted yourself and your staff in the effort to publish the best possible catalog, letters like those are heartwarming and encouraging. Among my favorite customers of all time was the lady who called to apologize for ordering only one item, not two or more. She didn't want to hurt our feelings, she said. Kudos or complaints, my son David and I read the letters, and every letter gets an answer.

I like suggestions from customers. Someone once wrote and suggested that we sell flannel sheets. My son Fred also urged me to sell them, so I put them into the catalog, and they were terrific sellers. A long time ago, another customer saved us from a real gaffe. For years we had been carrying a book called School Years, intended as a parent's record of all a child's years from kindergarten to graduation. With each grade level, there was a page on which children could check off what they wanted to be as grown-ups. We hadn't looked inside this book for years. To say the list was old-fashioned is an understatement: The boys' checklist offered professions like astronaut, soldier, baseball player, policeman, and doctor. Girls had a choice of nurse, teacher, mother . . . I'm surprised we didn't have receptionist on that list, too. We are grateful to the customer who pointed out our oversight. We redesigned the book, and it is still in our catalog. Now the lists are in tune with today's career choices.

Another useful query came from a customer who wrote to tell us that she bought a lot of presents from our catalog for her nephews and nieces but sometimes had trouble figuring out what present was suitable for which age group. Could we help her? Since then, our copy includes age guidelines. After all, only parents know exactly what is right for a kid—aunts, uncles, Grandma, and Grandpa may not.

I'm always on the lookout for ways to cement my relationship with customers. Every issue of the catalog includes a letter alongside my picture. One evening in 1976, Fred and I were having dinner with my old friend Peggy Ryan, who worked at *House Beautiful*. Suddenly, Peggy said, "You should write a short note and put it with your picture in the front of the catalog."

"Oh, I couldn't do that," I answered. "It's an embarrassing idea."

Fred agreed with Peggy. They kept on about it, and finally, they persuaded me. I write about the company, about what's in the catalog, even about my family. Our customers like it, and I do think it makes the catalog more personal. I'm proud to tell you that even Hillary Rodham Clinton says that she takes the time to read my message. In an address before 250 leading businesswomen, Ms. Clinton referred to us, saying that "Lillian Vernon was always my favorite catalog." And, she added, "I also always faithfully read her message. It was encouraging about what we could do to get our lives in better shape. But also because of the example and the leadership, seeing her picture really meant a lot to me."

But what if, in spite of all the work and effort, orders are late arriving from our suppliers and therefore late going out? We do our best to let our customers know what has happened rather than letting them stew about their orders. Our policy costs us extra money, but the reassurance it gives the customer is worth it. Now government regulation mandates that customers be apprised of every order that will be more than a month late. We were way ahead of the government.

Customers sometimes have special requests. One may say, "I'd like to order the blue and green tablecloth. But if you're out of it, would you pick out the appropriate color for me? My dining room has pale yellow accents and just a touch of pumpkin," and our chief customer-service specialists will try to fulfill the request.

Gifts for Our Customers

On the sixteenth anniversary of our catalog, we celebrated by giving our customers a free gift with their purchases. Since then, gifts have been a staple of our marketing strategy. We don't give gifts simply to encourage orders, but because many times we give them in multiples—customers have choices, the gifts act as incentives to increase order size. The gifts range from the decorative to accessories to useful household items. I'm a great note taker and scribbler, and I'm always running out of pretty paper. So we offered notepaper as a gift. In 1981, we packaged sheets of various attractive colors with matching envelopes. That gift was a great hit, and lots of people ordered more of the notepaper from the catalog.

Another time we offered our customers three tiny tins adorned with old-fashioned postcard designs. Laura Zambano, our executive vice president of merchandising, and I had hunted for samples in the Paris flea market, in New York's SoHo district, and on King's Road in London. When we couldn't find exactly what we wanted—more than one million sets of three—we took the idea to a manufacturer in the Far East. We designed and developed exactly what we wanted. Six weeks later, back home, we had received nothing from the manufacturer—not even a sample. By New Year's, we still had nothing, and I responded by doing what I do best: I panicked. I was due to leave on a buying trip three weeks later, and waiting until my return to solve this problem was unbearable. Then luck came my way. At a housewares show in Chicago, I ran into an old friend who had once been one of our suppliers. He had made us a charming kid's lunch box many years earlier. I explained our crisis to him. For cash up front, he would fulfill my requirements. So I went ahead and, miraculously, before my departure he delivered. He made new tools, created silk-screen designs, and rushed the job to completion at high speed. We bought 1.2 million tins from him. As I've always said, Only in America!

We promote our gifts, and the response has always been excellent. One year, we decided to stop giving those gifts. When our customers complained and our sales went down, we discovered that the gifts do, indeed, enhance sales.

Some mail-order houses use sweepstakes to bring in customers. We have never done that because we feel it does not fit our image. On the other hand, in a limited way, we have used discounts. In 1973, to customers who wrote in asking for a catalog, we offered a first-order 10-percent discount. Current customers didn't get that offer. We found that the discount didn't seem to make a difference, and that proved something that I've believed all along—it is the quality of the catalog and marketing to catalog shoppers, not gimmicks, that brings in orders.

My parents.

I'm in the baby carriage, with my parents and
brother Fred.

Baby Lillian.

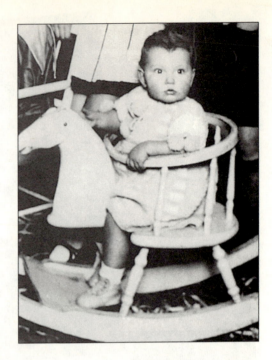

My brother Fred and me.

My first day of school, in
Leipzig, Germany.

Be *FIRST* to sport that

Personalized
Look
on your
BAG and BELT

Your very own 2 initials in 24 KARAT
GOLD, Embossed **Free** on this GENUINE
LEATHER Shoulder Bag with stunning
metal medallion, saddle stitching and
matching initial belt.

COLORS: Red,
"Honey", Suntan,
Brown, and Black

MADE TO ORDER

BAG $2.99

Plus 60¢ Fed. Tax

ADJUSTABLE $1.99
BELT

No Tax

VERNON SPECIALTIES CO.
16 Mt. Vernon Avenue, Mt. Vernon, N.Y.
PLEASE SEND ME: ____Personalized Bag @ $2.99 & 60¢ Fed. Tax $3.59
____Personalized Belt @ 1.99, no tax 1.99
TOTAL...$5.58
PRINT INITIALS _____ COLOR _____
Can be ordered separately. If middle initial is desired add 25¢ for each bag
and belt. □ Check or money order. (Postage paid). □ I enclose $1.00
deposit. Send C.O.D. plus postage.
Name _____
Address _____ City _____

The ad that launched Lillian Vernon Corporation, which
appeared in the September 1951 issue of *Seventeen* magazine.

With my sons Fred and David.

My first trip to China with Laura Zambano, executive
vice president of merchandising.

Visiting the markets of Hong Kong.

My first meeting of the White House National Business Women's Council.

With former New York
City Mayor Ed Koch.

Paolo Martino and I with New York City Mayor Rudy
Giuliani, after seeing Donna Giuliani perform in *La Traviata*.

Visiting President and Mrs. Clinton at the White House.

My sons, Fred and David Hochberg.

My home in Greenwich, Connecticut.

9

ALL THE WORLD'S A CATALOG

Return to My Roots

—

White Trees Glow in China

—

Life's a Banquet

—

By the early 1970s, it was time to take another big step, and the most logical was to go global. It was becoming increasingly difficult to find unusual items in the United States, and American consumers were developing a taste for exotic products. One of the keys to a successful mail-order business is having products that others don't, or that are simply hard to find. We had scoured the U.S. handicrafts industry for extraordinary gift items, and now we planned to do the same abroad.

Not that selling imported goods was entirely new; we'd been buying from importers for some time. But in 1972, we made the decision to import on our own. I started by visiting trade fairs in Paris, Milan, Hanover, London, and other European cities. A few years later, I extended my travels to the Far East—Hong Kong and Tokyo first, then mainland China in 1980.

As a youngster, I'd observed foreign cultures, and I'd trained myself to try to understand them, to accept different ways of behaving and reacting. Now, wherever I traveled, I learned quickly and was able to establish lasting ties with agents, vendors, and manufacturers.

Return to My Roots

Returning to Germany in 1972 was one of my most emotionally challenging trips. I arrived in Hanover for the country's annual products show—a major commercial event in Europe. But no sooner had I arrived than I found myself flooded with feelings of pain, anger, and fear. What was I doing in Germany? Was this trip a betrayal of my parents? My father once went back to Leipzig to look at his property. His feelings about what had happened were so strong, he wouldn't even sleep in Germany. He saw what he had gone to see and then took an overnight train out of the country. My Israeli relatives persuaded me to make the trip. They said that there were two reasons why I ought to return to Germany: first, I was a businesswoman who needed new products; and second, just as it's important not to forget, it's important to forgive. I couldn't help thinking, as I walked the streets of that ancient city, of my family's flight, of my brother Fred's death, of the nieces and nephews I would never have, of the uncle my sons would never know, of the family friends who had not escaped. It was a hard lesson, but I was able to face my feelings and reconcile them. I will never get over my brother's death in 1944, but I have made peace with the pain it has caused and with my feelings about the country of my birth. It helped that I was still at home with the German language and the cuisine. The taste of bratwurst, herring, and other quintessentially German dishes brought back happy memories of my earliest childhood.

White Trees Glow in China

Richard Nixon, shepherded by Henry Kissinger, made his surprising trip to Beijing in 1972 and opened the Chinese market. On a spring buying trip to Paris in 1979, I read in the *Herald Tribune* that Americans favored trade with China, four-to-one. For years, the ratio had been one-to-four against. That was a real change, and it persuaded me to follow in Nixon's footsteps.

The idea of visiting China, a vast and unfamiliar country, was exciting. Other than the food, which I loved, I was totally ignorant of China's current culture and its history. A local bookstore supplied me with an armload of material to begin my education. Among many other things, I learned that the Chinese—although they have a tradition of isolationism and a suspicion of foreigners—have historically controlled a great deal of the commerce throughout the East. If they are so commercially minded, I should be able to do business with them. In 1980, after many failed attempts, we finally organized our trip, obtained visas, and were issued official invitations to the Canton Trade Fair.

Armed with a little knowledge and a lot of hope, Laura Zambano and I set off that October to search for wonderful new products to sell. We felt like pioneers because we were among the first U.S. companies to establish commercial ties in China.

Our first stop was Hong Kong, where I was to meet Michael Tam, a young man who had sent us pictures of wicker baskets he wanted to sell through our catalog. Initially, we ordered 500, but we ended up selling 80,000, not a bad start for our first Chinese import. We still carry many of its offspring today. Michael had also mentioned in his introductory letter that he was establishing himself as a merchandising agent. As it turned out, he was attending the October trade fair in Guangzhou, so we flew to meet him.

We arrived at night, and I'll never forget the haunting and surreal approach as the plane descended. The Chinese wrap their trees in an iridescent white material that keeps insects away. My first vision of China from the window of the plane was of hundreds of white trees glowing in the warm darkness. It was astonishingly beautiful. Then, as the plane started to bank for landing, I realized with confusion and horror that there were no lights on the runway. It wasn't until a minute or two before we touched down that the runway lights flared to life. It was an unnerving introduction to a tantalizing country, my first experience of the non-Western world.

Once we were off the plane, the Chinese officials questioned us endlessly, scrutinized our papers and our possessions. I had read that the average Chinese owns only two sets of clothing, so we came with two garments each. Though we had brought the minimum, everything we had passed by the carefully watchful eyes of uniformed men and women armed with submachine guns.

It was there, at the airport, that we met Michael Tam. As soon as he greeted me, I knew I would hire him as my trader in China. His handshake was firm and strong, his English near-perfect, and he radiated confidence and intelligence. I felt absolutely certain—my golden gut sent a message to my brain—that he was someone I could trust, a man who would work for us with single-minded dedication. He has proved me right.

We spent four days at the trade show, looking and buying, with Tam as our translator. Some of the Chinese businessmen I met spoke German, and that made communication much easier. The schedule we followed was grueling: up by 7:00 A.M., five hours at the fair, lunch between 11:30 A.M. and 2:00 P.M., back to the fair until 6:00 P.M., a business dinner followed by an early bedtime. The whole trip was an adventure into another world. I learned something new every day. I long ago discovered that the only way to learn is to keep quiet, look, and listen. When I wasn't working, I soaked up as much of the culture as I could.

The fair itself did not disappoint us either. It offered an exotic display of goods: brass and bamboo ware, porcelain, ornaments of silk and satin, adorable hand-crocheted pandas, garden tools, rugs, and flannel sheets. The fair offerings were a catalog in themselves. On that first trip to China, we ordered twenty-nine items. Within two years, our business there amounted to some $2 million. Today, we do more than $10 million annually.

Life's a Banquet

As my company grew, I spent as many as four months of every year visiting trade fairs. I traveled at least 100,000—sometimes even 200,000—miles annually. Even when we searched in the mountains of Mexico for unusual jewelry, I was able to keep tabs on business. I received regular reports from home on the day's orders and shipments. I'm a firm believer that one should never—for any reason—be out of touch with one's business.

Visiting trade fairs is fun and exhilarating, but traveling abroad is particularly exhausting. I usually bring one or more merchandisers. We begin at 8:30 A.M. and spend nine hours walking back and forth through the aisles, searching. We examine quite literally tens of thousands of items and have to make decisions on our feet. When I'm lucky, I find the perfect item quickly, but that doesn't happen often. The times it has happened remain in my mind. I was once at the Frankfurt fair with my son David. We stopped at a booth displaying thousands of mugs. Tucked at the back of the bottom shelf, I spotted a little brown ceramic mug. It had a lightly speckled surface that gave it a wonderfully unusual look, and it came with a lid to keep hot drinks warm. I asked the price and ordered 10,000 of them—all in less than three minutes. Those mugs turned out to be terrific sellers.

On those trips, we can never put our feet up. Because we spend evenings with our business friends, talking about everything *but* business, our days don't end until midnight. My co-workers and I did develop one tradition that buoyed us up during those trips. Every trip, we'd all go out for a special dinner together—just us—to eat the best food and drink the best wine. Then, at the end of the meal, we'd ask the waiter to remove the labels from the wine bottles. Everyone signed the labels, and they became treasured mementos of our triumphant merchandising forays.

It isn't just at fairs that I have had to make major decisions very quickly. In 1976, we had one of those recurring crises. Based on a sketch, we placed an order for plates from Germany. We had planned to make the plate the cover of the Christmas catalog, but when it arrived, we saw that the manufacturer had changed the design, and no one liked it. In its place, we substituted a glass angel made on Murano, an Italian island located near Venice that is famous for its centuries-old glass-blowing industry. The angels—made of multicolored millefiori beads—were lovely. The angel on the cover was such a huge success that we quickly realized our original order of 3,000 would never suffice. We needed at least 10,000 more to satisfy our customers. Fred, David, and I went to Venice together to try to solve our problem. We boarded the little boat—a vaporetto—to Murano, where we met with the manufacturer. He had interrupted his vacation for us.

When I told him why we'd come, he shook his head in dismay. "Signora, signora," he said, "I don't have enough ovens to fulfill your order before Christmas."

"I will get you the ovens," I told him.

We went to Germany, where we bought ovens and had them shipped by air to Murano. Still, our manufacturer had to hire extra workers, and those, according to Italian law, he would not be allowed to lay off once demand dropped. Then and there, we made a deal to continue to give him orders. In the years to come, we bought paperweights and miniature glass Christmas trees from him. Since then, we have built a lifelong business relationship and a lifetime love affair with Italy.

I was very touched by one experience I had in Germany at that time. From a glassmaker in Berlin, I had been buying small stained-glass windows. When the glassblower died, a woman called me and told me that she would be continuing his work. "He told me," she said, "that you depended on him for your business, so I feel it is my duty to continue to help you." All that time, he had really believed that his glass work—I bought only about 1,000 pieces from him annually—had kept me going, and she was determined to keep up the supply.

I learned something very important during those magical buying trips. I learned to look after my health. When I started back in the 1950s, I had no money, and I scrimped on everything from hotel rooms to food. Then, as Lillian Vernon became more and more successful, I still economized foolishly. A safe and clean hotel was important to me, so I stayed at the best. Then, guilty over the cost, I would watch the cost of meals, taxis, and any little luxuries. I finally came to realize that keeping myself in good shape for the long days at the fairs was a legitimate expense. I was worth it. We all were. I started to eat well, and I made sure I got enough sleep. A special treat was a massage or some personal shopping time. It was part of growing up: a process of treating myself with the same respect I try to show others.

Even today I can't stay away from fairs. They keep me fresh. The challenge of finding just the right merchandise for the catalog, the horizons that a fair offers, the give-and-take with vendors, the chance meetings with old friends in the business, the trends you can pick up: all those activities stimulate and invigorate me. I have a real need to see what's out there. On a recent flight to Chicago, when the flight attendant recognized me, she upgraded my seat to first class. That sort of thing never fails to thrill me. It reminds me of how far the little immigrant girl has come. But much as I love to eat at four-star restaurants, the truth is I'm just as happy with a slice of pizza on the run. I enjoy it all. To paraphrase Auntie Mame: life's a banquet, and I've never lacked an appetite for anything.

10

OUR LISTS, THE LIFEBLOOD OF MY BUSINESS

How Do We Get Names?

—

Best Prospects

—

Expanding the List

—

Farewell to File Cards

—

Advertising for Names

—

From the time I began my business until today, I have expended energy and money on my mailing list. Bankers believe that our physical plant and our computer systems are our main assets but they are mistaken. It's our list. Lists are vital to the prosperity of a mail-order company—they are the basic building blocks.

Today, the Lillian Vernon list is computerized and sophisticated, but its beginnings were modest. I sat at the yellow Formica table in my Mount Vernon kitchen, laboriously noting customer names and orders on index cards. That was our primary list; people who had bought from our early magazine ads.

I'll never forget the effort involved in fine tuning that first list. Every two months I would stay up late weeding, pruning, adding, and subtracting. I had to keep it current. People move, stop ordering, get married, get divorced. We estimate now that we lose about 20 percent of our names annually. That means that expanding the list—our unwavering goal—requires increases of slightly more than 20 percent annually. In this business, you just cannot rest on your laurels; if you're not moving forward, you're slipping behind.

Duplicates are the bane of any mail-order company's existence. How often I sat up, bleary-eyed, until 3:00 A.M. huddled over a pile of 3"-by-5" cards trying to figure out whether Catherine Smith, Mrs. Catherine P. Smith, Kate P. Smith, and Mrs. Kate Smith—all living in the same apartment building—were the same person, four different people, or some combination of the above.

When we began our catalog in 1960, we already had 125,000 names. I don't know how other people in the business start up; they may rent lists from other mail-order companies or they may build lists gradually, as I did. By the early 1980s, our list had more than ten million names. In 1997, we're above nineteen million. We mail out eight different catalog titles each year. To maximize efficiency of the mailings, not every customer gets every catalog.

It gives me great pleasure to think that some of those first customers, the teenagers who bought my bags and belts, are now grandmothers who still buy from us. Year after year, for more than four decades now, many of the same people have continued to order from Lillian Vernon. Customer loyalty makes a firm foundation for a mailing list.

How Do We Get Names?

We tailor each of our catalogs to a specific market, and we try to make sure that our lists reflect the tastes and needs of that market. Contrary to what many people think, a company's lists don't originate from such sources as country-club rosters, criss-cross directories of affluent neighborhoods, Junior League registers, college alumni memberships, exclusive stores, United Way contributors, or telephone books. Those lists are far too random to work for the mail-order business.

It is true that the more names on the lists of a mail-order company, the higher its sales volume will be. So why not just send catalogs to everybody? Wouldn't such a mass mailing be a surefire way to increase sales?

Here's why that approach doesn't work. A company might well generate additional sales by random bulk mailings of catalogs, but it's crucial to watch the bottom line as well. Catalogs are expensive to produce and expensive to mail. Hence, scattershot mailings invite catastrophe. No one could stay in business that way.

YOUR CRUCIAL LISTS

In any mail-order business, the customer list is the most valuable asset. When you first begin, excellent customer records must be a priority. Record the name and address of everyone who buys from you and, most important, what they buy, what they spend, and when they reorder. Someone who reorders is a customer. I began my list on index cards, then on Addressograph equipment, but now it is computerized and much more sophisticated. In the early days, I considered name, address, and date of order to be adequate. Now, mail-order lists include such data as occupation, age, sex, marital status, education, and income level. All that information helps us target our buyers.

It may seem strange that mail-order companies rent and trade one another's lists—in other words, share their customers. This is now an accepted way to expand lists. We rent these lists for one-time use, but once someone on the list has made a purchase, that customer is legally ours. As your own list grows, other mail-order companies will want to rent your names, and list rental can be a significant source of income. The Direct Marketing Association in New York City can put you in touch with list brokers when the time comes.

Best Prospects

Some companies have a policy of aggressively pursuing only affluent customers. Many mail-order businesses specialize in high-ticket items, and they rationalize that the well-heeled are those most likely to purchase their expensive products.

MARKET RESEARCH

The mail-order business does its own market research. You send out a catalog with, say, one hundred products—eighty sell and twenty bomb. You drop the twenty quickly You really need to do market research before you start your business. First, decide which segment of the market your product appeals to. Who should your customers be? I started with a product designed for teenagers and aimed my first ad specifically at them. If you plan to sell skiing equipment, don't open your business in Florida or put your ads into magazines for older people. If your products are toys, then advertise in children's magazines or magazines for young mothers; *Parents* or *Parenting* are good choices. A thoughtful marketing strategy can focus your advertising. Use publications that reach your target market. There are so many specialty magazines available today that no matter what you are selling—herbs, health-food products, sports equipment, or shoes—you can find a suitable publication. You just need to go to your newsstand with a fistful of dollars and buy them.

Match your product to your potential customers. You can get a good demographic breakdown by age, income, and employment from U.S. census figures. Write the U.S. Census Bureau in Washington, D.C., or consult your public library to help find those statistics.

Before your company sends out a catalog, you might want to use focus groups to test customer reactions. I have found the experience very valuable.

My approach has always been different. In keeping with my conviction that customer loyalty forms the backbone of a list, I have looked for people who have already bought by mail—no matter what their income. When I go to look for new customers, I hope to find people who have developed the habit of buying from catalogs. Our early customers were women who had already bought belts, purses, and jewelry from me. I knew that they would be better-than-average prospects for catalog shopping. First and most important, they bought by mail. They had proved they weren't put off by the idea of purchasing a product they hadn't actually held in their hands. Second, they were likely to have an interest in the kind of merchandise we were selling. Third, they were my customers, so they knew that Lillian Vernon was a reputable mail-order company. An established, recognized name is one of the biggest assets in our business. Friends have told me that people wait for the Lillian Vernon catalog to do their Christmas shopping. A reputation like that is priceless.

Bearing in mind the high value we set on customer loyalty, we divide people into those who don't usually buy by mail and those who do. We appeal to the first group and try never to lose a customer from the second. I have also discovered that the more often people buy by mail, the more likely they are to keep on doing so.

While the prime prospect is someone who shops through the mail, it's important to know what kind of merchandise a customer is likely to order. From the start, I knew that my best prospects were women. I designed my catalog to fit their tastes, factoring in age, lifestyle, and past purchases.

Expanding the List

Because the growth of my company depends on increasing the number of my customers, I have been—right from the beginning—alert to new names. I found most of mine, at first, through magazine ads and the all-important word-of-mouth. Since we began mailing a regular catalog, I've always included a card that asks our customers for the names of other people who might also like our catalog. Our order forms still ask for those referrals.

When the phenomenal expansion of the mail-order business started in the 1970s, acquiring names by trading or renting lists from other companies became one of the chief means of procuring names. Shortly after publishing my first catalog, I started to rent our names to other companies and rented names from them, or we traded them. It may seem self-defeating for mail-order companies to share their customer lists with their competitors. But that's exactly what happens. When we rent a list, we make sure that every person on it has ordered by mail at some point in the past. Then, if our catalog merchandise appeals to them, we have a good chance of making a sale and acquiring a permanent customer.

There are lists, and there are lists. I would never rent a list from a company whose merchandise is incompatible with mine, badly made, or in bad taste. Lillian Vernon sells merchandise to women. We aren't going to spend money renting the list of a men's clothier or the list of a company specializing in power tools. If you sell CDs, it wouldn't be the best idea to acquire the list of a company that sells mountain-climbing gear.

We also stick to a price range that's in line with our own. You don't pitch a Rolls-Royce Silver Cloud to the Plymouth Neon crowd.

Farewell to File Cards

When our company rents a list, the first thing we look for is the date of a customer's last order. Current customers are the most desirable. Thanks to the latest technology, all leading mail-order companies can give us this information. The computer can keep track of a range of customer activities. I couldn't put any more information on my 3"-by-5" cards than name, address, and most recent order. Nowadays, we can cross-reference all sorts of helpful data. We know who has bought toys during the past six months, who has spent more than $100 on merchandise in the past year, or who has made two or more purchases in the past eighteen months. By what she buys, we can even pinpoint a customer's merchandise preferences: Is she a gardener? Is she a cook? Does she buy a lot of ornaments? Is she a grandmother who buys toys and children's clothes at Christmas? We store all manner of invaluable data on the computer. We are able to offer other mail-order companies specific lists tailored to their marketing needs, and they can do the same for us.

When we receive a list from another company or rent one out, it comes in the form of mailing labels or magnetic tape, and the borrower pays a specified fee for the right to do a single mailing. It's strictly a one-time transaction, and everyone understands that it's a breach of contract to send a second mailing to any of the names on the list—except to a customer who makes a purchase from that first mailing. Once that happens, the customer's name automatically joins the renting company's list.

Ours is a close-knit industry, and companies are reputable. Since acquiring other companies' lists is such a vital part of the mail-order business, a company that gets ostracized because it doesn't live by the industry rules will, in the end, do itself irreversible damage: word about dishonesty spreads quickly, especially on mailing list use.

Before making a major commitment, it's wise to test another company's list a few times just to make sure that it meets our needs. Lists are expensive to rent, so I prefer to test them step-by-step. We test by taking a cross section of names, say 10,000 or 20,000, and seeing what the response is. Once we know how much money customers from that test list have spent, we calculate the total number of dollars spent per thousand mailings. With this information, we can figure our breakeven point as well as the margin of profit. We may then test a second time and mail to 25,000 and a third time by mailing to 50,000 or 100,000 names. If we get a good response, we'll go ahead and buy several hundred thousand names from that list.

You would be amazed at how accurate our statistical projections can be. By testing 50,000 names, we can project our sales—using additional names from the same company— within 10 percent. With larger tests 300,000 names, projections are even closer to actuality, and we can estimate sales within a 5 percent margin of error.

The price of a list varies, depending on a company's requests. The more specific the list, the higher the price. Depending on what a company is looking for, lists go for as much as $100 per thousand names. The closer you target your specific audience, the higher the price goes.

When we rent a list, we also have to make sure that we're not duplicating names. We take care of this problem by a process known as *merge-purge*. If we rent lists from ten different companies, we could conceivably end up sending as many as ten catalogs to the same person. In addition to being expensive, this kind of sloppy overkill can alienate customers: current and potential. Let's say that we rent one hundred different lists, totaling ten million names. Everything goes into the computer. First we make each list compatible with our own, and we produce a report on duplicate records. Then, of all the names from all the companies, and from the ten million names we started with, we end up with five million names that we can actually use.

I once heard about a company that worried its market could become saturated if it rented its list. Customers, it felt, might be inundated with catalogs, leading to a decline in its own sales. So the company divided its clientele into three control groups. During a twelve-month period, the names in one group weren't rented, names in the second group were rented to six companies, and the third group's names were rented to twelve companies. The test revealed that the more catalogs people received, the more they responded to the original company's own catalog. Management concluded that its fears were unfounded.

An important specialist in our industry is the list broker. A list broker brings the seller and buyer together. In a sense, a list broker functions like a stockbroker or a real estate agent.

Advertising for Names

In addition to acquiring names from other mail-order companies, our primary list builder, we also procure names through advertising in such handpicked magazines as *House Beautiful, Better Homes and Gardens,* and *Smithsonian,* as well as *Woman's Day* and *Yankee.* We chose those magazines because we believed their readers were most likely to respond to our merchandise. We maintained a year-round advertising schedule, and we tailored each ad to the individual magazines. We could afford such a variety of advertising outlets because we carried so many different products at a wide range of prices. Some of our items cost $1, others cost $70. Customers can buy for the kitchen, the garden, the closet, the nursery, and every other room in the house. We carefully analyzed the demographics of each magazine and advertised accordingly.

Image matters. For that reason, we pick our advertising outlets with great care. We never use newspapers, and we avoid mass-circulation media, whose standards do not match our own. Neither of the above targets the specialized audience we look for, and magazines have a longer life. That is one reason why we selected lower circulation but specialized publications. It's a way of honing in on our audience.

Our ads offer a free catalog to everyone who makes an

inquiry. You can order it through our 800 phone number or by writing us. To cover handling charges, some companies ask the customer to send money—usually $1 to $5—for their catalogs. They reason that anyone who responds is a prime prospect because he or she is willing to pay for the catalog. I don't believe in charging. To me, that's like a department store charging customers to come in to shop. Bloomingdale's doesn't collect an admission charge from customers who browse—and neither does Lillian Vernon.

Each order we ship contains a catalog, and we suggest that our customer pass it along to a friend or relative. When a satisfied customer gives the catalog to an acquaintance, it's bound to have a positive impact. In effect the customer is saying: "Here's where I shop. I recommend it highly." I've relied on that kind of word-of-mouth endorsement since the days when I sent out my simple four-page black-and-white brochures.

Our lists are so precious that to make sure nothing happens to them, we copy our files onto magnetic tape. Once a week, we remove the tapes to a safe offsite storage facility. And, of course, we back up those all-important files.

Some mail-order companies put the customer's name and "or current resident" on their catalog address labels. We do not. "Current resident" says to the customer: "We don't care if you are there or not, we just want to make a sale." That isn't an image we want to project. It's too cold and impersonal. I believe that the personal touch is what matters in the mail-order business.

11

AGENTS, VENDORS— AND FRIENDS

Friendly Vendors, Unscrupulous Rivals

—

Reordering

—

Woks in the Basement, Beetles in the Kitchen

—

Creating the Catalog

—

The Pictures and the Words

—

Fulfillment

—

The Price of a Good Story

—

When I began trading overseas in the early 1970s, I was once again extending my boundaries and following the instincts of an entrepreneur. My motto has always been: Never stand still. As I sought out new opportunities, I also always calculated the potential risks. What risks were involved in obtaining merchandise from abroad? It didn't take long for me to realize that the key to achieving success and minimizing risk lay in having reliable agents and sources: representatives you can trust.

I picked mine the same way I chose most of my key employees and products—with an eye for winners. My first agent in Italy, one of the countries where we do a lot of business, was an Austrian. He came to work for us in 1972. His name was Manfredo Danzig, and he had been taken to Italy as a prisoner during the Hitler era. He was a super agent and a grandfatherly friend, and when he died in 1978, we were doubly bereft. Now the hunt was on for a replacement who was as trustworthy and as likable. We knew it would be a difficult, important task: all signs pointed to continuing growth in our business in Italy. At the time of Mr. Danzig's death in 1978, we were importing $600,000 worth of Italian merchandise—everything from leather handbags to glass bottles and solid-brass candlesticks.

We interviewed candidates in Milan, Rome, and Florence. I spoke with more than fifteen people. Fred, Laura Zambano, and her sister, Norma, a vice president of merchandising interviewed others. Still we couldn't seem to find the right person, and it was beginning to look as if we'd never discover a replacement. Then, in Milan, we got lucky. Dario Laus, the Italian buyer for Marshall Field's, had written to us in December 1978 saying he was thinking of leaving the company to open his own office. We cabled him back, saying we'd like to talk to him. In January, he joined us for a walk around the Milan toy fair; and going from booth to booth, I watched as the vendors greeted him with genuine warmth and trust.

We went back to our hotel for a drink at the bar, and I took out our current catalog. I pointed to the bottles and jars we'd photographed for the cover.

"Do you know who manufactures these?" I asked.

"Egizia," he answered at once.

I looked at him and smiled. "You're the first person I've interviewed who's known the answer to that question."

Without a written contract from the company—just a friendly handshake—he left Marshall Field's and joined Lillian Vernon on June 1, 1979. We opened a handsome new office in Florence, our first outside the United States. It's located on the Arno River between the Grand Hotel and the Excelsior Hotel. We didn't scrimp on the offices because— let's face it—Italians put great importance on what they call *una bella impressione*—a good impression. Our office is on Florence's Via Borgognissanti and has a terrific view of the Arno. We furnished it with the light, sleek contemporary furniture for which Italy is famous.

Friendly Vendors, Unscrupulous Rivals

It isn't just the agents you pick who are important in the mail-order business. Reliable vendors—the people you buy merchandise from—play an equally decisive role. I develop a loyalty to them, and they reciprocate. Once, one of my competitors was shopping for merchandise with a Lillian Vernon catalog in his hand, trying to knock off my line. My vendors thwarted him: one of them called to inform me: "Lillian, the only way I'll offer my merchandise to this man is if you aren't going to run it in your catalog or ads again."

His commitment stopped the competition in its tracks.

Whenever I found a product I liked at a vendor's booth, I factored in the shipping, freight, and duties with the other costs. In my calculations, I determined how many I'd need to sell in order to make a profit. The costs of buying in the United States include manufacturers' payments and shipping. When it comes to buying abroad, there are other expenses involved. You have to figure freight charges per cubic foot and U.S. customs duties. The arithmetic is like one of those math problems in a school exam. Thank God for computers.

Reordering

There are times, though, when certain items surprise us and really take off. A good example is the glass angel from Murano that we put on the cover one year. We expected to sell 3,000. Instead, we sold 13,000. I've had the good luck to be surprised in this way many times—starting with my very first mail-order bag and belt. Maybe that set the pace for the coming years. When something really takes off, we have to reorder, and coping with reordering is one of the trickiest parts of the mail-order business. I always make sure the manufacturer understands the way we do business. Orders usually start coming in by the fifth or sixth day after catalogs arrive in customers' homes, but we base reordering on a three-week assessment: by that time we can pretty well forecast our total sales. In China, where most of our products are handmade, the first purchase order has to hit the mark. That means figuring the numbers very closely, a nerve-racking process.

We always check very carefully on the quality of our merchandise, especially from abroad. Merchandise from the Chinese mainland is checked in Hong Kong. Our Italian merchandise is checked in Italy. All our merchandise is also carefully scrutinized before we put it into the catalog. Is a toy safe for children? Will a shawl lose its color in the wash? Can a plate withstand a dishwasher's heat? We have special labs to test our merchandise. Our employees often take kitchen tools home to make sure they live up to the manufacturers' promises. We refuse to sell anything I don't know inside and out.

Woks in the Basement, Beetles in the Kitchen

We have had some pretty hairy experiences with merchandise from abroad. In 1965, I had to store thousands of woks in the basement of our house. (Although I hadn't been to Asia, I was already doing some ordering from there.) The woks, it turned out, had made the voyage with hordes of beetles. Within days, the terrifying black creatures had over-run the whole house. We had to engage an exterminator who specialized in unusual pests.

Another time, we ordered toy pandas from China for our Christmas catalog. They were almost as adorable as the real animal, but—horrors!—when we opened the shipment, the toys were moldy. Somehow they had gotten wet in transit from Hong Kong. We threw out the entire shipment and had to explain to customers what had happened.

Only after brass candlesticks we had ordered to give as free gifts arrived from Italy did we discover that their bases broke off. We sent the entire shipment to our Providence plant, strengthened the bases, and replated each candlestick. My good friend Marty came to the rescue again. The Italian manufacturer had been so intent on meeting the delivery date that the shipment had not been thoroughly checked out.

As well as buying at trade fairs, we often go directly to manufacturers. We do that when I discover a product—a lamp, a wine rack, a paperweight, china, anything—in a store

BUYING ABROAD

As your business expands, you will want to travel worldwide to search out merchandise. People often ask me how one pays for the merchandise. The easiest way is to open a letter of credit from your bank. The seller deposits it, but it is held in escrow in the manufacturer's bank. When the manufacturer can show a bill of lading to prove that the order has been shipped, the bank releases the funds. In some cases, we pay against an invoice when goods are ready to be shipped.

Also, you will probably want to buy samples as you visit trade fairs. Plan what you will need, and take along enough cash in travelers' checks to cover expenses. As foreign vendors get to know and trust you, they will extend you credit market wide.

or in someone's house, and I want to feature it in the catalog. Today we have companies manufacturing for us all over the world.

Creating the Catalog

Back in the 1960s, when we had one sixty-four-page catalog, the job of preparing for publication was simple. At least it seems simple compared with the procedure we go through today.

As the time approaches to prepare our newest catalog, the samples we've ordered come pouring in. We record each sample, a tiresome but necessary procedure that has given us a lot of headaches. We tie on labels that note the cost, the source, and the day of arrival. It's even easier today because we have automated the procedure, recording everything in an electronic notebook. Every day, I get a list of what has come in, and I check it carefully. We may have twenty basket samples on hand, but because five baskets in one catalog are plenty, we'll make some serious choices.

Once all the sample merchandise is on hand, we have what we call our selection meeting. These events often seem like free-for-alls because I want everyone present to voice likes and dislikes. Friends of mine in the business instituted a system for choosing catalog items that I always considered perfect. They had a merchandising team of three: the boss and two buyers. If they all agreed about an item, no problem. If the boss and one buyer agreed, also no problem. If the two buyers agreed and the boss did not, then the buyers had exactly five minutes to convince the boss that they were right.

At Lillian Vernon, the merchandising staff, our chief photographer, the art director, and the copy chief all take part. All of them have strong—and sometimes contradictory—opinions. We discuss how we see an item in the layout, our reasons for picking it, and how we should price it. Our final decisions are—well, final. There is a generous right of veto, and my rule of thumb is that if anyone truly detests an item, we should forget it. Conversely, if someone adores an item, even though others do not, it still has a good chance of making it into the catalog—we always have some winners that way: the soft sculpture people, for example. They are five-foot figures representing anything from a leprechaun to Uncle Sam and Santa Claus. And we've had some losers that everyone adored. As for those—I prefer to forget them. The mail-order business is a game of Russian roulette in which winners are ultimately determined by that intangible factor called customer response.

We spend a lot of time examining and discussing each candidate for the catalog: Should an item be monogrammed? Does it measure up to our standards? Once we had to reject a lamp. It looked fine in a sketch, but when the sample arrived, it proved to be unstable and unsafe. Another time,

Laura Zambano and I had picked a handsome porcelain pot intended for steaming chicken. We had both managed to overlook the lack of a steam hole. I guess neither of us does much steam cooking. My son Fred, who knows a thing or two about cooking, tested the pot and put us right. At our selection meeting, we all agreed the pot was too handsome to reject: we decided to sell it as a server instead.

Once we know what items the catalog will include, we move on to the next step.

"Let's discuss the hand-turned wooden ornaments from Spain," I say.

"They'll photograph well," comments the photographer.

"We've got ten samples here, so you pick the five that you think will photograph best," I tell him.

Then we may go on to discuss colorful woolen gloves from Turkey, which Laura Zambano loves. I like them, but the photographer and art director feel lukewarm about them.

"At $9.98 a pair they're profitable," I say, "but they won't sell well at that price. We'll put them in for $7.98 and make up the margins by adding something to another item." A penny here, a penny there—it all works out.

I know why the art people are not enthusiastic about the gloves. They don't lend themselves to interesting photography, nor will they look as eye-catching on the page as the wooden ornaments. Laura and I win this one, though. And so it goes, from German Christmas-tree ornaments, to Italian leather handbags and belts, to a decorative clock from Japan and at least five hundred other catalog candidates.

Sessions like this can go on for days, and they occur all through the year. We put together entirely new catalogs every month of the year. The catalogs can run to 120 pages and feature as many as 700 items. We publish eight catalog titles: *Lillian Vernon* (1956), *Private Sale* (1982), *Lilly's Kids* (1990), *Christmas Memories* (1992), *Personalized Gifts* (1994), *Lillian Vernon's Kitchen* (1995), *Neat Ideas for an Organized Life* (1996), and *Welcome to the Best of Lillian Vernon* (1997).

Choosing the items is only the first step. Once we know which will go into the catalog, we do layouts, approve them, and then have everything photographed. How should we present each item on the page? Sometimes the photographer will come to us and say that he can't figure how to make something look good. We have to suggest different angles, different lighting. We ask a lot of our photographers because we do not want to retouch color transparencies. We don't use sketches. The customer gets what she sees—sometimes even more than she sees. I get many letters that say, "I'm pleased and surprised at the quality of what I ordered. It's better than I expected."

Despite all our efforts to show our products to the customer as honestly and explicitly as we can, we still sometimes run into problems. In 1982, we had a handsome purple poncho in a catalog that unfortunately photographed with a bluish tinge. We got a letter from a schoolteacher who wrote, "I would have bought your poncho but, although the caption said it was purple, it looked blue in the picture. I can't afford to take a chance." That's the kind of catalog pitfall we strive to avoid.

Depending on the season, we decide on the number of pages in the catalog. The length can vary from 48 to 120. Then we sort the items by category: housewares, toys, games, products for the kitchen or the bathroom, teen spreads, garden spreads, gifts, back-to-school pages, men's gifts, and decorative items. Organizing the catalog that way makes it easier for customers to find what they want. A friend once told me that my catalogs look as organized as my closets.

The Pictures and the Words

Together with the art director, creative staff, and buyers, we spend days trying various arrangements of pictures and copy.

We mix new items among the old. Sometimes we highlight one product of the eight on a facing page to create a spread. We don't put expensive items on one page and cheaper ones on another. A page of bathroom items may have a toilet brush for $7 and an unusual extension mirror—with seven rather than only five arms—for $20.

The next step in producing the catalog is writing the copy. We try to keep the copy as straightforward and factual as our photographs. For the first sixteen years, I wrote copy myself. Now we have many copywriters, but the style remains the same—no exaggeration, no hype. We stick to straightforward description. After that, we fine-tune every detail—right up to the moment the last page is out the door.

For many years, we made it our policy to sell only exclusives, but in 1981 we changed that. It was a major decision. After thinking it over, we decided that it really didn't matter that others might be selling long-handled feather dusters, too. It was good business to carry them on our household pages. That way, our customers could order the dusters from us—instead of a competitor—along with all the exclusives they wanted. We based our decision on the realization that as the catalog grew—we now carry more than 6,000 items—we could not develop enough exclusive items and do it well. Our mix of exclusives and excellent, useful, and attractive nonexclusive products has increased sales dramatically.

Fulfillment

Everything we do—from merchandising to the publication of our catalog to taking orders—culminates with order fulfillment, one of the mail-order challenges and opportunities. The process of receiving orders, logging them in, and then sending order forms to the warehouse used to be tortuous and error-prone. Now, with phone orders so common, the problems have been reduced. Still, slipups sometimes occur. Misspelled names, bungled addresses, incorrect order details, wrong sizes: any one of those errors may mean a return. Nowadays, with modern technology, we can fulfill orders within a few days. We ship five million packages annually— more than twenty million items—pretty much error-free. We began with our first computer back in 1975. As we expanded, we also used an outside support service. When the big crunch came in the early 1980s, we were caught short and spent two years installing the latest customized technology. We learned the hard way that sometimes too much business can be as bad as too little.

We've programmed our computers to catch errors. If the item number on an order and the dollar amount don't match, the computer rejects the order. If an item can be personalized and the order does not call for monogramming, the computer lets us know. This quality control at the front end of the fulfillment chain corrects a lot of potential mistakes. Every day I find another reason to respect our technology. It is expensive, but it is irreplaceable.

We have quality control in the shipping department. We keep running accounts of our warehouse inventories; our people examine merchandise carefully before they package it; and we do spot checks of packages leaving the warehouse to make sure they have been packed correctly. In fact, 99.6 percent are!

Our shipments vary from 50,000 packages in a slow week to as many as 360,000 a week during our peak periods of Christmas and Halloween. Such a load can make fulfillment a challenging job. We have asked our fulfillment department to handle some tough assignments. Enamel rings, which came in eight colors and five different sizes, could be ordered from the catalog in groups of three or six with unlimited choice of size and color. The fulfillment department rose to the challenge, and the item was a winner for years.

TECHNOLOGY

As your company grows, so will your need for technology. A personal computer will serve your early requirements. As you grow, so will your need for more sophisticated systems, and your costs will mount correspondingly. In the 1980s, when the Lillian Vernon Corporation expanded so rapidly, we had to acquire a system with a price in the millions. Our previous system simply could not carry the amount of information we were putting into it.

Today, mail-order businesses can advertise on the World Wide Web, which is a whole new way of getting a message out—and letting customers respond. However, I don't advise anyone who is not yet well established to undertake such a venture.

The Price of a Good Story

The mail-order business is at the mercy of glitches that can make mischief anywhere in the process, from acquiring our products to getting them to our customers. A manufacturer falls behind, and our deliveries are late. The shipper—UPS, Federal Express, or the U.S. Postal Service—can run into weather problems. Blizzards in the Midwest can tie a delivery schedule in knots.

One time, we were anxiously awaiting a back order of 5,000 barbecue implements. Finally, to our relief, the truck pulled up to our loading platform. However, when we opened the trailer, we found it filled with cooking ladles. The wrong trailer had been hooked to the truck cab. Another time, a shipboard crane snapped and dropped a crate full of glass angels. The dock sparkled with the tiny shards of broken glass. In the mail-order business, you learn to roll with the punches. We have also created our very own glitches. Our February cover in 1979 featured a beautiful set of brass scales. It became a hot seller, so we ordered another shipment from Italy. What happened? Because of high seas, several containers were dumped overboard, and ours were among them. In retrospect, disasters make for a great story, but you have to learn from them if you're going to survive in this business.

12

A SECOND MARRIAGE

Venturing into the Art World

—

A Family Business

—

More Family Business

—

I'd been divorced for six months when I met Robert Katz. On February 28, 1970, some good friends of mine encouraged me to attend a party with them. By chance, I made my entrance accompanied by the husband. Robbie saw us and assumed the happily married man and I were a couple. He made his way over—"just in case," he later told me—and introduced himself.

Robbie was a tall, handsomely built man with a warm, captivating voice and a charming sparkle in his eyes. He had a thoughtful and intelligent look. Here is the kind of man I could love. As soon as we realized we were both single, our halting conversation shifted gears, and the mating dance began.

I called my mother the next morning and told her that I had met a man I could marry.

It's always a pleasure to feel that a man is attracted to you, and the pleasure is doubled when you're also attracted to him. We both enjoyed dancing, and in those early days of dating we often stayed out until 4:00 A.M., whirling across the dance floor. Robbie presented me with a lovely yellow sapphire engagement ring, and we were married on October 24, 1970, eight months after we met. It was a simple ceremony. Fred and David gave me away, and we limited the guest list to family and the couple who had introduced us.

Robert Katz was twelve years my senior, a recent widower after a twenty-nine-year marriage. Suave and urbane, he had the social ease that comes with affluence and education, and he was secure enough in himself to encourage me in my pursuits. Trained as a professional engineer, he had turned to business—first the manufacture of air pollution devices and later, with my encouragement, Lucite products. Those kind of men bring out my funny side. He made me feel amusing and witty, fun to be with. Perhaps most important, he made me feel confident and bold in my business dealings. He encouraged me to go ahead with whatever plan I believed in. I wasn't used to such support, and it made me feel secure—and loved.

My life took quite a turn. It was a lighthearted time, which I look back on with great fondness. Dinner parties, nights on the town, a pied-à-terre in Manhattan: those features defined the shape of our marriage. At the same time my company was exploring foreign markets and getting into the import business. Sometimes, to my great delight, Robbie joined me. He accompanied Laura and me on an early buying trip to China, and we went to trade fairs together in Europe.

Shortly after we were married, we bought a house in Mamaroneck, a rambling place large enough for my two sons and Robbie's son, Stuart, and daughter, Ronnie. After living there for six years, we moved to the house where I still live, in Greenwich, Connecticut. It's a beautiful home with a pool and a pond on three and a half acres, only thirty minutes from my office.

I decided to furnish the house, whenever possible, with products from my catalogs. Kitchen equipment, items for the bathrooms, lamps, bowls, candlesticks, sofa pillows, dishes, closet hangers: I chose all of them from the products I offer my customers. When I couldn't find an item I wanted—certain kinds of dishes or lamps—I tracked them down, bought them for myself, and added them to the catalog. I loved living with the very products I found for my customers. If, in the course of using an item, I discovered flaws, I searched for a better-made, more reliable replacement for the catalog.

Venturing into the Art World

That was the time I started to take some pleasure in purchases entirely unrelated to business. On a buying trip to Mexico in 1972, I called the gifted Mexican painter Rufino Tamayo. To my surprise, his number was listed in the phone book. Around noon on the day I was leaving, I went to his studio. There I saw an oil painting, executed in watermelon pinks and greens, of a man standing in front of a tree. The title was *Jesus and the Cross*.

I fell in love with the painting and immediately wrote a check for more than $23,000. Tamayo, who had never met me before, accepted the check without hesitation. His trust amazed and touched me deeply. When I left, he kissed me good-bye. Many years later, his beautiful work of art continued to please me.

I also started to collect English silver. That began in 1983, when I was in London on a business trip. The graceful lines of a pair of eighteenth-century Queen Anne tapered candleholders caught my eye. The owner of the shop offered them to me for $3,000, but I demurred. "I can't buy them," I told him, "because I don't know anything about antique silver." I then set out, as quickly as possible, to give myself an education on the subject. I consulted books, experts, and knowledgeable friends. Two days later, when I called up the store owner to say I wanted the candleholders, he informed me they'd been sold. I was not deterred by my first loss, and eagerly continued my studies. I visited every antique silver shop in London and asked questions. I found that there was a tax on silver in eighteenth-century England, so the silver dating from the reigns of Queen Anne and the three subsequent King Georges is light. Victorian silver, from the nineteenth century, is heavy because the government lifted that tax. Armed with my new expertise, I began to acquire my collection of antique silver.

A Family Business

My two sons were well on their way to maturity when I married Robbie. Fred was eighteen and starting college. David, at fourteen, was still in school. Both boys attended

Hackley in Tarrytown, New York. Fred was a good student, but David hated academics. Fred was so taken with the centennial of the Metropolitan Museum of Art that he decided to major in art history at the University of Rochester. Like any other mother, what I wanted most for my children was their happiness. But in my heart, I must admit I had hoped to pass the company on to one or both of my sons. Even when they were very young, they had helped me. As children, they grew adept at opening the mail and rolling up quarters for bank deposits. As teenagers, both boys worked at the company over the summer. I guess that even when they were young, I was trying to instill in them pride in the family business.

Just when Fred's interest in art seemed to point him away from the company, he transferred to New York University to major in business. He graduated with honors and went on to get an MBA from Columbia University. By that time, I was perhaps becoming impatient. I wanted him working at the company, but he insisted on finishing his master's degree first. I now see the wisdom of his decision. He was right.

Fred joined the company in 1973. Because he had worked there when he was young, many of his co-workers called him Freddy, and I think that may have been difficult for him at first. He was careful on the job never to call me Mom. I was always Lillian or Mrs. Katz. It amused me to hear Fred greet me with "Good morning, Mrs. Katz," when I met him in the hall. I was so happy to have him working with me that I failed to foresee some of the problems that would arise.

When David was in college, he had no interest in business. He wanted to be a journalist. That was during the Watergate era, and like so many people his age, he was determined to fight for justice and to expose hypocrisy. David is completely forthright. He says exactly what's on his mind, a trait I admire—even when it makes me cringe.

He attended journalism school at George Washington University, but like me, he left two years before graduating.

I invited him to join me on a buying trip to Italy. He was a fine companion and showed good business sense, spotting several items for the catalog and making on-the-spot decisions about their potential profitability. On that trip, I saw a side of him I'd never noticed before. He has a relaxed attitude toward life he inherited from his father. We had a great deal of fun together.

More Family Business

In 1978, we started a wholesale division that sold such specialty gifts as exotic soaps and herbal vinegars to boutiques and department stores. We rented a showroom at 225 Fifth Avenue in New York City, a wholesale gift center, and we needed someone who could work with the architect and eventually run the operation.

I used that challenge to lure David into the business. At first David was reluctant to work with his brother and mother, but because he showed a flair for management, I thought he was perfectly suited to run his own division and be his own boss. When it became clear that he would have control, he agreed.

By 1979, David was confidently running the show. To avoid confusing customers, we called the new line Provender. As the Provender Company developed, we opened showrooms across the country, and in a few years we no longer needed expensive Manhattan real estate. We closed the showroom, which had become costly to operate, and moved the offices to our Mount Vernon headquarters, where David maintained his business. Maybe it was because of that arrangement, but he never had a problem calling me Mom at work. Provender produced its own handsome catalog for its wholesale trade. It featured soaps, body lotions, sponges, toothbrushes with multicolored bristles, and even champagne toothpaste.

During that time, Fred often found himself playing the role of troubleshooter. Somehow, when anything went wrong, from advertising to fulfillment, people would call on him. It meant that he could never really concentrate on one project at a time within the company. He wasn't happy in that role, and I can see now how frustrated he must have been.

Finally, he got some good advice from our auditor: "If I were in your boots, Fred, I'd earn my spurs by tackling the company's biggest problem: fulfillment."

In 1972, we bought our first major warehouse, a large facility in Mount Vernon, and it didn't take us long to outgrow it. Outgrowing warehouses has become one of the constants of my business. In 1978, six years after we opened our Mount Vernon facility, our business growth forced us to buy a 100,000-square-foot warehouse in Port Chester, New York. In 1982, we rented another building in Elmsford, New York. Fulfillment is always a complex procedure, which needs a lot of attention to function smoothly. The Port Chester facility ultimately was a bottleneck and a headache for all of us, not only because it was, in time, too small, but also because the location provided an inadequate labor pool. For ten months, Fred worked at that warehouse until he knew every aspect of its operation. He got his hands really dirty, and when he had gotten everything running smoothly, he returned to headquarters with a sense of genuine accomplishment. That's when I started to groom him for leadership of the company.

In 1981, there was a need for a formal marketing department, and I put Fred in charge of it. We had never had a separate marketing function before because we had counted on the catalog alone to increase our orders. If we mailed out 1,000 catalogs, our average response was 25 orders. Now we hoped to increase the response rate to 30 or 35 per 1,000. Fred and his staff worked to promote the Lillian Vernon name. They suggested we adjust certain prices, pointing out, for example, that in our Christmas catalog we offered too many items at $3.98 and not enough at $4.98. (A customer with a $5 limit on Christmas presents is often willing to spend that extra dollar.) Fred also insisted that we encourage customers to pay with their credit cards, which would make things simpler for them and for us. In 1973, customer orders averaged $10; by the end of 1995, the figure had ballooned to $49. That's quite a hike!

Our advertising department, which fell under marketing, was also Fred's responsibility. Our four-color full-page ads enticed customers with such slogans as "Come browse with me in the little boutiques of Europe," and "Chinese jade, French Limoges, all at Scottish prices." Those ads did a lot to push us into the forefront of the mail-order business.

I was really pleased to have both my sons working at Lillian Vernon and doing well at their jobs.

In 1986, we decided we had to build another distribution center. After considering various options, Fred and I decided to investigate Virginia Beach. We each spent a week there trying to get a feel for the place: I walked through shopping malls, went to the movies, and checked out the supermarkets. Would it be a good spot for our business? Fred and I scouted possible locations in the area where we could have as many as fifty acres. At a meeting on our first day in Virginia Beach, a representative of the Hampton Roads Development Authority said that the lowest price he would accept was $50,000 an acre. Earlier, at a dinner meeting in New York, they had inadvertently let a price of $20,000 slip out. But Fred, Kathy Tenenholtz, and I had been paying close attention and had absorbed the lower quote. When we started negotiation, we reminded them of their original price, told them that it was as much as we could afford, and pointed out how many jobs and how much extra business we would bring to the area. Finally, they accepted. The lesson here is that it's always important to keep your ears open and stay alert. Sometimes an unexpected set of lucky circumstances simply falls into place.

Negotiations in foreign countries are often full of surprises. In Taiwan once, Peter Morton was negotiating the price of an item when a fax arrived from my office. As I read it through, I felt increasingly frustrated, and I exclaimed angrily, "I've had it!" To my astonishment, the Taiwanese businessman suddenly spoke up, saying "Any price you want—anything! I don't want to upset you!" Of course I accepted his offer, never acknowledging that what had caused my irritation was having to deal with a recurring problem from my office back home.

Fred assumed the complex and demanding assignment of overseeing the design and construction of the new Virginia distribution center. He directed the building of a handsome glass-curtained two-story, 486,000-square-foot facility. It allowed us to consolidate four of our operating sites. We encountered our share of problems along the way, mainly with the floors: to move large packages with laser-guided machinery, the floor must be absolutely level. We moved in on May 5, 1988, and started operations in time for the holidays. By the beginning of 1989, the Lillian Vernon Corporation could boast one of the most up-to-date plants in the direct-mail industry. State-of-the-art technology accomplished almost every aspect of our operation: monogramming, labeling, bar-coding, and packing. And Fred did it all for under $25 million, our largest single investment up to that time. No one else could have done it as well or as efficiently. It was a true labor of love, and I'm deeply grateful. Regrettably, I believe that Fred never heard my gratitude: a parent's criticism often sounds louder than praise.

As I've often told my friends, I may have been the one to start with a dream and a line of handbags, but Fred and David were the ones who brought my dream into the modern world. They kept on top of the latest technological developments and brought them into our company: a state-of-the-art distribution center, the use of credit, deferred billing, and toll-free ordering, to name a few. We've had our share of tough times, but we've endured—as a family and as a business. Each of my sons has a bedrock commitment to quality and to the highest ethical standards. We've grown up together, with many tears and much struggle along the way.

With both sons finally in the business, it was time for me to relinquish some of the daily work.

13

BACK FROM THE BRINK

My Million-Dollar Mistake

—

Consultants

—

Hiring from Within

—

Nightmare

—

Picking Up the Pieces

—

From the Ashes

—

Entrepreneurs who have founded and run companies naturally look upon their business enterprises as their own special creations, as if they were their children. You can't run a big, successful company, however, without loosening the reins, and that's not always easy to do. It feels a little like letting a beloved child go out into the world: you know you have to let go, but it's very painful.

I had always done everything and been everywhere. When a crisis threatened, I would be the one to solve the problem. I was the company firefighter and the company cop. If there was a problem in the warehouse, I was the one who called the warehouse manager, or rushed over to take care of it personally. I never signed a check without reviewing the bill. Every morning, I was the first in the office. And I approved every line of catalog copy, deciding that we were overusing the word *fun*, or were being precious when we described a product as *precious*. Yet I still do that. After all, with my name on the cover of the catalog, I'd better know what's inside.

Sometimes, after hours, I answered the phone and spoke directly with my customers. They were amazed to find me on the line listening to their complaints. Who, after all, can tell you more about how you're doing?

I really had nobody to teach me the ins and outs of big-company management. Most people gradually work their way up the corporate ladder, learning from other executives. But I didn't have managers who could act as guides and mentors. I had to teach myself.

If my company had continued to grow as slowly as it did through its first nineteen years, I might have had the luxury of growing slowly with it. But it didn't happen that way. In the years between 1970 and 1984, the Lillian Vernon Corporation grew from a $1 million business with a relatively small clientele to a $115 million business with customers nationwide. We went on to grow between 12 and 13 percent annually throughout the decade. That is a phenomenal expansion.

I know it sounds wonderful, but rapid growth brings with it terrible strain. As many consultants pointed out, I had a tiger by the tail. Without warning, I suddenly had to change from being an entrepreneur to being a manager and administrator. I needed different skills. A manager's job is essentially to keep the company running smoothly day to day, to cope with crises, to keep track of information accumulating in databases. I had to learn to be a hands-off entrepreneur. My company's future growth depended on my personal capacity to grow and change.

Learning to manage was tough. I needed professional management in a hurry. Following the accepted path, I hired MBAs, "experts" in management, but what a mistake that was. In my experience, most people with MBAs are not on the same wavelength as entrepreneurs. Although I could supply the necessary entrepreneurship myself, I still wanted people in the company who could make decisions on their own. Instead, those MBAs carried analysis to the point of paralysis.

After disappointing experiences with the MBAs, I increased my involvement in finding good people. It wasn't hard to hire good managers, but I had to learn how to give them leeway and make sure that they used it. I told them, "Don't expect me to second-guess you. Success or failure is up to you." There's no point in hiring able people if you don't give them a chance to use their abilities. With the responsibility squarely on their shoulders, people learn to act decisively. I have always looked for another me. If I found that person, I reasoned, my company would be twice as good.

Growth brought yet another problem to the company. From the very beginning, communication among all of us

FINANCING GROWTH

Growth often calls for an infusion of capital. Even if you have accumulated cash resources, you may still have to approach outside sources to cover expansion costs. If you have run your company alone, now is the time you might look for a partner who will bring in an infusion of cash. There are various options open to you: Approach a manufacturer with whom you have worked. Talk to investment bankers. Consider a merger with another company in your field.

No matter which option you settle on, you may have to change the legal status of the company— from sole proprietorship, perhaps, to a limited partnership.

You might also approach the Small Business Administration. The SBA works through commercial banks to guarantee at least a part of a loan. With the SBA's guarantee, banks are more receptive to your petition for a loan. Remember, though, that an SBA-guaranteed loan involves plenty of paperwork, which includes detailed reporting on all your expenditures.

If your business is growing quickly, venture capitalists may be interested in making an investment in exchange for a large slice of equity. You should understand that venture capitalists look to make a large profit, expecting to move in and out of their investments within the short term. To assure the investors' liquidity, the small company that takes venture capital will need to either go public or be acquired. Furthermore, many venture capitalists take a management role in their investments. Certain entrepreneurs find such a relationship intolerable.

was excellent. In 1972, there were eight staff managers sitting in two adjacent offices. Even if you didn't want to listen, you could not help but know what everyone else was doing. With the mail room on one side and fulfillment on the other, there were no secrets at the Lillian Vernon Corporation. By 1983, we had 650 people working in five different buildings, and keeping open lines of communication throughout the company had grown increasingly difficult, if not impossible. The staff members were becoming strangers to one another. If we wanted to project a friendly, warm image to our customers, friendship and warmth had to exist in our workplace. This was one of the knottiest problems I faced.

I began by holding regular meetings with the executives. We brainstormed for ideas, discussed company philosophy, and analyzed procedures. I believe that those meetings were responsible for much of our growth, for they gave the participants an overview of what was going on in the whole company. The success of the meetings depended on an informal give-and-take. As the company continued to grow and we added personnel, there were simply too many participants to maintain the old informal atmosphere. When we broke the meetings down into two separate groups, operations and marketing, we lost important feedback and communication.

In the mid–1980s, we tried a different approach. First, we asked each executive to prepare an informal but informative memo each month: How had the department fared? Had the department tested any new ideas or approaches? What plans did it have for the coming months? The memo was really a family round-robin letter of sorts, chatty and newsy. That plan did what it was supposed to do: it kept everyone in the company up-to-date.

Our second approach to the communications problem was much more radical. We decided to take a close look at a number of key positions in the company. As a company grows, there's a tendency to create new departments. The easiest solution for overworked executives is to add staff ad hoc. Such measures lead inevitably to a top-heavy organization—a situation I definitely wanted to avoid. So we made the decision to try to rely on outside resources and services whenever we urgently needed more help. I fought to keep communication free and easy, and I succeeded.

In 1980, I made a decision that might astound some executives: to stop growth. We needed time to sit back and analyze the company's structure and needs. How would we cope with our unexpected and sudden growth? We devoted that year to shoring up our operations. Revenues still increased a robust 25 percent—really more than we could handle. Our computer systems, warehouse, and workforce simply couldn't deal with the volume of orders coming in. We worked around the clock. It was usual for me to be in the plant until midnight, but even that wasn't enough. We ended up spending a lot of money on UPS second-day air freight. And to customers who still didn't receive their orders in time, we offered a full refund. Customers who decided to keep the late shipments received a half refund. It was hard and expensive to make and keep these promises, but customer satisfaction has always been the bedrock of Lillian Vernon.

I should have taken it as an omen when, in 1981, I ran into trouble launching a new catalog called *At Home*. Targeted to a specialized market, and featuring such items as a $425 sofa bed and a $300 coffee table, *At Home* was supposed to be an upscale version of our main catalog. Even though we produced an exceptionally handsome catalog, the venture was doomed from the very start. Our customers did not look to us for sofa beds and furniture.

My Million-Dollar Mistake

The economy was part of the problem. The country was in deep recession. People had no cash for major purchases.

What's more, we launched the catalog after Christmas, thinking the timing would enhance sales. To our dismay, we found that people had already spent their extra cash. In our rush to roll out the new catalog, we failed to buy the right mix of products—genuinely original and unusual items from Europe and the Far East. To top it all off, I had given control of the catalog to a manager who carelessly let errors get through. I had obviously delegated too much to the wrong person. Finally I stepped in and stopped the whole project. We lost about $1 million. I realized later that I had to take full responsibility for bad planning.

I had failed to follow my own rules. I hadn't overseen the merchandise, hadn't analyzed the market. I had relinquished control and I had delegated fully without making sure I had chosen the right person. The furniture we carried was too pricey, and because it was quite heavy, our shipping costs were high. We offered a blue-tiled porcelain stove for $1,800. Our rugs carried $1,000 price tags. Paintings cost up to $2,000. We even carried a $75 pen, an item meant only for people for whom cost was not a consideration. Those aren't the kinds of products that encourage impulse buying, which is often the response to casual catalog items. By moving into a field that did not have the Lillian Vernon personal touch our customers had come to recognize and respond to, we had gone badly astray.

I have always been able to close doors without regret because I know that there will always be others I can open. So when I dropped the *At Home* project, I said, "All right, what's next?"

Thank goodness all flops aren't failures. I recall a buying trip to England in 1978 when I happened to come across a warehouse full of antique wooden sewing bobbins. I fell in love with them and bought the entire lot, some 80,000, to use as a gift for those customers who spent more than $15 ordering from our upcoming February catalog. When the bobbins arrived at the warehouse three months later, I was horrified to discover that there were small ones and large ones and therefore were too costly to ship as gifts. So I decided to sell them. I put them on the cover of the April catalog, priced at $3.98 each. They sold out in three months. We had originally ordered two shipping containers of the bobbins. When we realized how big they were, we canceled the second container. Now we had to do a turnaround and reorder the second one.

Consultants

I didn't want a company with many-tiered management, so I used consultants whenever possible. If I didn't think they were right for my company, it was easy to change the relationship. I have discovered, however, that choosing consultants still requires care. Some just want to keep you barefoot and pregnant—dependent on them forever. I was lucky to find really talented people. That meant, of course, that I had to weigh their advice against my inclinations and knowledge. Sometimes I took their advice, but I confess that at other times I went my own way. The results speak for themselves.

I found a new accounting firm, Coopers & Lybrand, who claims I hired them for their sense of humor. They were probably right. There aren't many people who can find anything funny in statistics.

Hiring from Within

Besides turning to outside consultants, I have tried to promote from within the company. Choosing associates is a tricky business, and I have always trusted character more than education. I like working with people who know the company and have a feel for the way we operate.

I remember when Ray Slyper first came in 1973, as an

assistant in our list department. She was only twenty-three years old, with a high school diploma and not much self-confidence. What she had in abundance was a passion for hard work, an extraordinary eye for detail, and a truly infectious laugh. She was gutsy and vibrant, and when she walked in every morning, the atmosphere in the office seemed to brighten. I adored her. The only thing I did not adore was her summer wardrobe. She used to report for work wearing jeans and a halter top, her midriff entirely exposed. One day I picked up a rhinestone button, and very carefully put it into her navel.

"Now you're dressed," I said.

She never wore jeans and halters to work again.

When we needed someone to become the head of our all-important mailing lists—the family jewels—I asked Ray to do it.

At first she hesitated. She was afraid to take on so much responsibility. But she agreed and did a great job. She became a vice president and major contributor to the business. She finally set out on her own and has been very successful. Work has always been an important part of her life. She even met her husband, Michael Bryant, at a business-related party.

There were others who rose in the company. Laura and Norma Zambano came to work in 1978. The two sisters have great style and an admirable zest for life. Although their parents were of Italian descent, neither of them grew up speaking Italian. When Laura prepared to accompany me on a buying trip to Italy, she enrolled in Italian classes, where she learned enough to help us with purchasing. Later she became a catalog coordinator and then an associate vice president in merchandising, and Norma took on responsibilities as a manager for merchandising. More than anything, I valued their extraordinary sensitivity to and understanding of the needs of Lillian Vernon customers and for their incredible eyes for graphics and products.

YOUR EMPLOYEES

Sooner or later, you are going to have to hire people to help you. You will probably do best at first to hire part-time employees, as I did. In most communities, mothers with young children are happy to work during school hours or do clerical work at home. Beyond that, there are certain qualities you should look for in employees. Good telephone manners are crucial. Someone who is abrupt on the phone may lose you a valuable customer. While your company is small, everyone will be working in close quarters. Look for people who are agreeable and cheery. We developed a real family spirit at Lillian Vernon in our early days, and I have tried to maintain that spirit with the 3,000 employees we now have.

Don't overhire. Spend time and effort on training people. In the end, they will appreciate the trouble you have taken to turn them into skilled workers.

Plan to pay above the minimum wage; if you insist on paying the lowest wages, you will find yourself hiring untrained workers. Of course, if you need only envelope stuffers, high school or college students may serve you well. For tasks that require initiative and self-confidence you will do better with experienced workers.

Before you begin hiring, visit your local employment office and ask about government regulations, or talk to a tax specialist. There are federal and state laws—they vary from state to state—covering employment. For instance, any employee, other than one who works at home, is subject to payroll deductions. As your company grows and you hire a larger and larger staff, you will have to cope with more and more laws and regulations: the Equal Opportunity

Act, the Americans with Disabilities Act, and a host of others. If you are selling food of any kind, your local health department will inspect your cooking facilities.

All of these regulations call for mountains of paperwork. You can try to take care of everything yourself, but based on my experience, I urge you to turn this chore over to an accountant. An entrepreneur's time is better spent concentrating on the business itself.

It may seem premature to prepare an employee manual when you have only a handful of people, but in the long run it will smooth the path for employee relations. Your manual should deal with such issues as vacations, dress code, hours of work, and compensation for sick leave. To be sure that you don't inadvertently violate any regulations, you may want your lawyer to review your personnel policies.

Even though the number of our employees kept growing, I always tried to make sure they all felt they were working for a person and not an institution. I recognize extended service to the company with a five-year-anniversary sterling pin, a ten-year Tiffany watch, and gala dinner party. I write personal notes when people are sick, get married, or receive promotions. In 1983, when we had so much trouble getting all our orders out and had to refund customers, I had promised everybody a little something extra at Christmas. Our cash flow was a problem, but I never considered disappointing my employees.

I measure the success of my efforts by the number of people who have stayed with the company in double digit years. Their loyalty is a matter of great satisfaction and growth.

It's not only employee loyalty I prize, but customer loyalty as well. I'm thrilled when a celebrity who can afford to order from the priciest catalogs in the world chooses mine. I was delighted to discover that Frank Sinatra was on my customer list. He had ordered a monogrammed lint remover through the mail. I figured if Ol' Blue Eyes was shopping with me, he must approve of "my way." Many other famous people have ordered—from Barbara Bush to Hillary Rodham Clinton, from Brigitte Nielsen to Arnold Schwarzenegger and Betty White. But much as I value my famous customers, I get the greatest satisfaction from the millions of women—and men—who have ordered from our catalog over the past forty-six years.

Nightmare

In 1983, the Lillian Vernon Corporation had serious problems.

Many people may be surprised to learn that growth and profits are often incompatible partners. Sudden increases in orders require considerable cash and capacity, and it takes time for revenues to catch up. I found myself having to expand our facilities and add to the payroll. I consulted with advisers in labor relations, lawyers, and accountants: everything costs money, and expert recommendations do not always come fast enough.

The company had still another problem. All year, buying on a global scale, we ordered huge quantities and built up a massive inventory, which we couldn't move fast enough. To make matters worse, our obsolete computer system failed to keep up with an 80-percent increase in business: it couldn't take orders or print our labels fast enough. We used an outside service bureau for much of our computer work. Our fulfillment was dangerously slow. Updating the system would cost millions. What had been designed for a small company had to serve a business with revenues nearing $100 million.

We had expanded so fast that we were playing catch-up all the time—only we couldn't catch up rapidly enough.

I found myself in a hole. All my assets—some $20 million worth—were sitting in warehouses, and there wasn't nearly enough cash coming in. I couldn't pay my bills, which were

---

INVENTORY

One of your earliest and most critical decisions will concern your opening inventory: How much should you have on hand when you start? Keep inventories low: until you can project your sales, your inventory should be as tight as possible. Always be sure to track how much of your product you have on hand; your inventory is an invaluable guideline to the health of your company. It can tell you precisely what your sales figures are; it can keep track of returns; it can tell you the response time to your ads and what sells well at what time of year. Above all, it can tell you what items are good sellers.

Some small businesses have gone under because they have not kept precise count of their inventories. Remember that every dollar tied up in inventory leaves a dollar less for other business expenses, and the costs of maintaining inventory are high: they include product cost, insurance, and transportation in and out of storage.

Once you can project the sales level of any item, you should be able to figure your maximum stock level, your minimum stock level, and the optimal point for reordering.

A personal computer can really help you here. There is specialized software that can help you track the status of your inventory. Check your local retailer for the best model you can afford.

FULFILLMENT

Like a three-legged stool, the mail-order business has three main supports: merchandise and marketing, customers, and product delivery, or fulfillment. Fulfillment is your bridge to the customer. That may sound simple, yet it is here that unexpected glitches can trip you up. In my career, I have encountered every possible disaster—both large and small—but I have survived. You will too. Weather, strikes, and acts of God—earthquakes, floods, accidents, even cargo-boat sinkings—can disrupt the most efficient systems.

The easiest orders to process are those that customers place over the phone. At Lillian Vernon, we can get those shipped in two days. About 50 percent of our orders come in that way—the rest come by mail. Since mail orders entail opening letters and sorting them, fulfillment is not as fast, although we aim to ship within three days. The advantage of an 800 number is that it encourages more phone orders.

There are certain basics you must master if you want your fulfillment system to run smoothly. Teach your employees how to pack so that your product isn't damaged in transit. Order enough corrugated boxes so that you don't run out unexpectedly and ship late. Work out a reliable delivery system with your shipper, be it UPS, FedEx, or the U.S. mail.

Get the best systems you can afford, and the best possible employees. Attention to detail is the catchword here. If you let up on that, you may be saying "bye-bye" to your business.

no longer for $495 ads in *Seventeen*. I needed millions to stay afloat.

I told Robbie that I might have to fold the company.

"You always dramatize," he responded offhandedly, not believing me.

"How I wish you were right," I said.

I had never before been in such trouble. My sons, my employees, all felt like a crushing responsibility. Was it conceivable that all my work—the business I had founded, nurtured, built up, and kept going—would suddenly cease to exist?

I had grown up not knowing what the next day would bring. I'd watched Nazi youths throw my brother down a staircase. I'd seen my father build up more than one business from scratch. I'd been forced to learn new languages, make new friends, adjust to new cultures. Now, once again, I faced fears that recalled those of my childhood. In many ways, the business had saved my life: now I faced losing it.

Picking Up the Pieces

I wasn't used to debt. I had always paid my bills on time. But I was determined not to declare bankruptcy. If I could go to the bank to use an adding machine, then I could go to the bank to borrow money. I was sure the bank would rake me over the coals, and who looks forward to that? But I also knew that when I speak from my heart, people trust me.

My lawyer shored me up, too. He pointed out that I had a very sound company. When I told him that I would use my personal assets to dig myself out of debt, he rose from his chair and announced that he would refuse to represent me if I did that. I don't suppose he meant it, but it helped my self-confidence and determination.

I was nervous that day; accompanied by my lawyer Leo Salon and my son Fred, I walked into the bank president's office. There was no use stretching the truth: my company was in trouble, and it needed an immediate infusion of cash. The bank had my word on it: I was good for the money.

I got a $13 million loan, which I repaid months before the due date. We were able to pay our bills quickly as our busiest season started. We also contracted for the installation of a more sophisticated computer system that we customized to perform Lillian Vernon merchandising and operations miracles and fulfillment.

From the Ashes

We were out of debt and growing fast once again. Our orders were shipped on time; our inventory was down; and we'd paid off our debt to the bank. Sales reached over $100 million in 1986, and the time had come to secure our financial stability and expand further. I decided to take the company public. I would list the Lillian Vernon Corporation on the American Stock Exchange. My lawyers advised me against making that move so soon, especially while we were busy getting our new distribution center in Virginia Beach up and running. But I knew in my gut the time was right. I planned the initial public offering for August 1987. Again the lawyers recommended waiting: midsummer is a hard time to catch the attention of investors. But I was due to leave the country on a buying trip, and I wanted to get it done. "Do it now!" is a rule I live by, and it certainly served me well once more. If we had waited, the stock market crash of October 19, 1987, would have postponed our public offering for a long time.

We offered 1,900,000 shares at an initial price of $15. I remember the day vividly. It was August 14, and swelteringly hot, just as it had been more than thirty years earlier as I waited by the kiosk for that copy of *Seventeen*. I walked into the imposing stock exchange building with my two sons.

David didn't want to acknowledge why I was so keyed up, but Fred did. He understood what the occasion meant to me. I was making history by introducing the first woman-founded company onto a major stock exchange.

I was planning to celebrate the event with my family so we celebrated with Fred, Robbie, Michael Lynch, our investment banker from Goldman, Sachs, and my friend and lawyer, Leo Salon. Celebrate we did—what a special achievement for Fred, David, and for me.

14

HEARTACHE AND NO REGRETS

A Death in the Family

—

Troubled Times

—

The Lillian Vernon Corporation survived its crises, and through the 1980s and 1990s the company has grown more and more financially secure. Sales went from $126 million in fiscal 1988 to $173 million in 1993 and rose to over $196 million the following year. Our sales increased between 12 and 19 percent annually, with 80 percent of our items making money. We employed as many as 4,000 people during peak periods. We now have 19.4 million catalog buyers in our database.

During those years, we also expanded our retail outlet stores. By 1991, we had three: the first was in New Rochelle, quite near the company's original home. When we opened our distribution center in Virginia Beach, we added one store there and another at Potomac Mills, outside Washington, D.C. These outlet stores are where we sell overstocked items and those we do not wish to sell again. And we now have more than fifteen stores in New York, Virginia, Delaware, and South Carolina.

I like coming in to work, greeting everyone, chatting with employees and working with them. The atmosphere of the workplace has always stimulated me, and a good working environment is important to everyone. Our offices have always been airy, simply furnished, and very clean. I've had arguments with my maintenance supervisor about repainting. He would say, "We can't afford it," and I would tell him, "Never mind that, no one can stand the shabby look of those walls." My own office has always been organized and functional, qualities more important to me than glamour and high style. When I started my business, I didn't have a desk, let alone an office, and somehow I managed to get my work done.

I've found it hard to work in messy surroundings, but I

OPENING A RETAIL STORE

Many well-established mail-order companies also open retail stores. Some sell at a discount and others at full price. I opened my first one in the 1960s, and it was a success from the beginning. My company now runs over fifteen outlet stores plus seasonal stores. It's the best way to keep catalog offerings fresh, generate extra sales, and make a profit on leftovers.

You may ask why a company whose reputation is built on mail order also needs a walk-in shop. Retail stores are excellent advertising for the catalog. I have found that items that do not sell out in the catalog will sell in a store. Perhaps there are customers who respond more readily to an object if they can see it and touch it. Many mail-order firms are started after success has been reached first at retail. The merchandise is very compelling, and will attract a wider audience.

don't believe in spending company money on show. I don't need an office that exists to impress visitors. For twenty-one years, my office was in Mount Vernon. Then I moved to New Rochelle. There, I furnished my office with a desk, a handpainted screen, and a conference table. The table was from my old dining room set. The black chairs I found in a trattoria in the Italian seaside town of Porto Santo Stefano. They caught my eye during a luncheon visit to the restaurant with my Virginia friends Tommy and Gerry Nicholson, and I ordered them for the catalog. The screen was one I'd had at home for years: no matter how splendid the view from a window, I've always turned my back on it. My desk faces the open door of the office so I can see our bustling operation and be a part of it. I'm frugal and careful with company money and recycle whenever I can and I encourage my staff to do the same.

The business was progressing beautifully during those years, but shadows were darkening my personal life.

My marriage to Robbie faltered. His eyesight and hearing failed, and in his rage at life, he struck out at the person nearest to him: me. In 1988, we divorced.

One day, four years later, Fred came to my office and announced that he was leaving the company. I was unprepared for that blow, and I was devastated. What could I do but accept his decision? Even more painful for me to accept was his resolve to cut his ties with me completely. I must confess that I have never understood his need for such a radical step. It depressed me deeply. Two years passed before we became friends again.

A Death in the Family

My mother fell seriously ill in 1993. I knew she would fight, but at ninety-one years old, fighting wasn't enough. I was obsessed with ideas of healing and reconciliation. The thought of her dying without our ever opening up to each other saddened me inexpressibly. Whatever our differences, she was my mother, and I owed her so much. She had given me life, courage, honesty, backbone, and an example I have strived to follow. Surely that bond could bring us together.

My mother was an extraordinarily tenacious woman. She had always felt that our family was entitled to reparations from the German government for the loss of our home and business. Since Leipzig was in East Germany, it wasn't possible to file a claim until the country was reunified. It took years of fighting, but on September 19, 1993, two months before she died, her lawyer delivered a check for one million German marks (approximately $700,000). Sixty years after fleeing her home, her dream had come true. I called Bobby

Zrike, my banker at Goldman, Sachs, and asked him to open an interest-bearing account for my mother until she was better and could invest the money herself. Bobby, who knew by then that the women in my family like quick action, wasted no time, and the account started drawing interest even before the marks were converted into dollars. My mother never got to enjoy her hard-won restitution, but she was there to receive the check.

In the hospital, my mother longed for constant attention; she had two special nurses to care only for her, and even when she was in intensive care, she had a manicure and pedicure every day. I sat by my mother's bedside and gently rubbed her hands. She loved that. Perhaps this slight physical contact was a way of communicating our love. I've accepted my mother for what she was: a woman for whom warmth wasn't natural or easy. A product of a different world and time, she was constrained by the rigid conventions of her class. Perhaps she resented my bond with my father. Perhaps she resented my success. She's gone now, but the regrets remain, but so do the lessons, and all she meant to us.

I visited her every day before she died. I remember her innate elegance, her proud carriage, and her interest in the arts and literature. She survived many decades of widowhood with courage. How could I help but admire her? I also remember one of her funny little quirks. My mother loved ironing, but in the far-off days in Germany, when we had household help, she could not, as the lady of the house, be seen ironing. It would have been considered unfitting. When the desire to iron came over her, she locked herself into her bedroom and spent hours at the ironing board straightening every crease and wrinkle. It was probably as close to therapy as she ever got.

After she died, many old friends revisited and renewed old relationships. The doorbell rang one day, and to my great surprise and pleasure I saw two men who had worked for many years with Marty Waxman and me in Providence. Bill Carroll and Chris Antonelli were both big, important guys, and we used to tease them by calling them "the Bookends." Bill owned a metal-stamping plant; Chris, owned a gold-plating plant. I was so touched that they had gone to the trouble to pay their respects to my mother. It was a testament to the fond feelings many people had for her.

My own trials as a parent have increased my sympathy for my mother. Being a parent is tough, and there's no year-end balance sheet: just the vagaries of the human heart.

Troubled Times

My divorce from Robbie in 1988, my mother's death, Fred's leaving the company and breaking ties with the family, and David's announcement that he did not want to take over the company: all those heartbreaks took their emotional toll. I felt alone in the world. Sure, I could look with pride at my business success. I had enough money to live well. But somehow, the core reassurance I needed wasn't there.

To help me through those troubled times, I again turned to therapy—both physical and psychological. I consulted a therapist just as I had after the difficult period when Sam and I divorced. I remembered how helpful therapy had been then, and wholeheartedly recommend therapy to anyone who has to endure a devastating experience. For myself, at least, talking to a nonjudgmental therapist helped me regain emotional equilibrium. Physical therapy helped me, too. I began an exercise routine I've continued to follow for years.

I poured my energy into the company, always a form of therapy. Following disappointments and divorces, I was able to conquer some of my anguish by concentrating on work. It was good for me and good for the company. Although the Lillian Vernon Corporation was now manifestly secure, we still ran the company with no fat. We had a very lean team for such a big company. The mail-order business demands intense attention to detail. If an employee misspells a child's name on a coatrack, we had better be as concerned about it as the mother. Mistakes lose valuable customers. Everyone has to keep a sharp eye out for possible slipups, large and small. My presence in the office seems to increase everyone's vigilance. During those months when my personal life was in disarray, I spent long hours at my desk. I think it was good for me.

15

RENEWAL

The Test of Time

—

The Future

—

Forty-six years after taking $495 to start a very modest mail-order business, I am chairman of the $240 million Lillian Vernon Corporation. Time and success haven't slowed me down a bit: I still travel around the world searching for new merchandise, oversee the business, and put in long hours at the office. Always an early riser, I am usually at my desk by 8:30 A.M. I leave at the end of the day, along with everyone else. I can explain it only by saying that I love the mail-order business as much as ever. Still, this is a period of transition: I am planning to continue my full commitment to the creative, marketing, and merchandising sides of the business, while remaining chairman of the board and head of strategic planning. One of the big advantages of running your own business is that no one puts you out to pasture before you're ready to graze. As long as your mind stays sharp and your body fit, you can do as you choose.

Despite a general slump in the mail-order business—a reflection of a slump in all retail sales that began in 1991—my company is doing well. In 1994 and 1995, we enjoyed a 13 percent increase in sales. Sometimes, when people are really broke and can't afford a new car, refrigerator, or other big-ticket item, they buy small, interesting items so they'll feel less deprived. Even on a tight budget, they can afford to brighten up their seven-year-old's bedroom with a $24.98 goose-necked desk lamp in cheerful enamels. And Christmas, always our busiest season, seems resistant to recession. In 1992, the company's fourth-quarter sales increased by an extraordinary 16.1 percent over 1991. The following year, *Christmas Memories,* a new specialty catalog, on which I worked with Leslie Rossi, our vice president of specialty catalogs, debuted even better than we'd hoped, despite the economic downturn. It was a special achievement—most new launches take at least three years to break even.

Back in the 1950s, the mail-order business was largely in the hands of individual entrepreneurs like Max Adler of Spencer Gifts, Manny Greenwald of Greenwald Studios, and Leonard Carlson of Sunset House. They all started their own businesses on a shoestring. Later, they sold to large companies: Max Adler sold Spencer Gifts to MCA; Manny Greenwald sold to Charter Publications; and many of the medium and smaller companies merged or were acquired by giant corporations. While I knew I'd eventually want to lighten my responsibilities, I held fast to my company. My conservative accountant once said to me: "No one's going to buy you unless they figure they can make money. That being the case, why don't you hold on and make the money for yourself?"

His argument made sense to me. The company had given me wealth, independence, and enormous happiness and satisfaction. But in 1994, at the urging of my board of directors, I made the decision to sell. I had many regrets and some misgivings, but personal and financial factors seemed to indicate the right moment had come. The business was ready for a quantum leap with a strategic company.

The first offer came from a French company. (We called it the French invasion.) Although it appeared to be serious, the group was unwilling to match our asking price, and the offer failed. The following year, 1995, we embarked on serious negotiations with an investment firm. This time, it appeared the sale would go through. I had to steel myself emotionally. Was I prepared to sell? How much of my identity would I be trading away? What would my new life look like? It was truly a soul-searching time for me, a period in which I came to a deeper understanding of how much my business means to me, on every conceivable level. I spent hours with my therapist, analyzing the impact of the sale, and I agonized alone, long and hard. I'd wake up at 4:00 A.M. and

USING AN ADVERTISING AGENCY

How you word your ads is of paramount importance. A catchy phrase can make all the difference. You'll probably need to work with professionals to get something that really works. I wrote my own first ad, but it took me weeks to come up with copy that pleased me. In the end, I went to an advertising agency. They took the photograph of the bag and belt I was planning to sell, edited my copy, and did the mechanicals—the layout and pasteup. Even though this will cost money, it is worth it. Sometimes, for a small fee, an ad salesperson from your paper may be willing to help.

Call various agencies in your area to find out what they charge. Then meet with them and try to negotiate a beginner's fee. Just remember that you want your ad to be eye-catching but uncluttered. Make sure that the copy is enticing and that it does not send an overloaded message. I have always believed that hyping the value of a product is self-defeating in the long run.

pace around the house, desperately trying to fight off panic attacks. I had made a decision and I wasn't going to backtrack, but it was one of the most unhappy periods of my life.

Then, unexpectedly, the negotiations terminated. The mail-order business had become tough and risky: paper and postage costs alone had climbed 60 percent. The investment firm wasn't sure we'd meet its goal. I was in shock. For six months, I'd ridden an emotional roller coaster, attended more meetings than I could count, prepared myself for the sale of my life's work. I was left with steep legal bills and the memory of countless hours of panic and misery. It's like an impending wedding—you know you may have some tough times, but when the bridegroom doesn't show up at the altar, it's emotionally heartrending.

As a result of the negotiations, the people who had worked for me for years were also in turmoil. They worried about their future. What would happen to their jobs? No one can work up to potential under those conditions. Some left, and those who stayed needed constant reassurance. All of this added to my own distress and unhappiness.

Although I do not plan to retire, I do know that it's important to calculate the right moment to move aside and allow others to move up. "Exit strategy" is a buzz phrase in the business world. To me, that means that you can't stand still. You figure out your next move in terms of what is best for your company and for yourself.

The silver lining of that torturous time was a man named Paolo Martino. We had met several years before the upheaval in my business, and his support throughout was a sustaining comfort. Paolo is a strikingly handsome man. He was born in Italy, and has lived in the U.S. for over thirty years. He's an open-hearted man with a generous spirit and a contagious love of life. He sings while he cooks. He can always make me laugh, and sometimes—not too often—he can make me cry. Our relationship, unexpected and surprising as it was, has brought me great happiness and fulfillment, and a new appreciation for what I thought was merely a cliché: *joie de vivre*.

Before Paolo, my personal life and my business life were always intertwined: my sons have worked in the company, Sam did, and even Robbie was involved with advice and counsel. But Paolo is not a part of the Lillian Vernon Corporation. I've discovered it works better that way. During the tough sale negotiations, he was able to give me the love and encouragement I needed. And because he wasn't directly involved, he helped me look at events objectively. Without him, I would have struggled a great deal more.

I'm the boss of my turf, and Paolo is the boss of his. Among his many accomplishments, he is a remarkable cook and interior architect. When he's at work in the kitchen, I'm not allowed to enter. By now, you can probably imagine how upset I am by that rule!

Even though I still work hard, I have more time to myself, and I love that freedom. I feel as if I've given myself permission to savor the best of life. I haven't entirely shed my work ethic, but I have put it in its proper place. I can enjoy lunch with my friends without suffering guilt for wasting time, the way I did for so many years. I have a weight-lifting and aerobic exercise routine I follow five times a week and wouldn't miss that for the world. It makes me feel healthy and in control of my body. When Robbie and I divorced, I lost twenty-two pounds, and I have worked hard to make sure the weight has stayed off. As one gets older, it helps to keep fit and look young, instead of giving in to the pull of gravity. I have had plastic surgery, and I feel it did as much for my spirits and self-esteem as it did for my face.

My activities, interests, and philanthropic work are more extensive than ever before. As a company, the Lillian Vernon Corporation has always been generous: we give to some five hundred charities every year. I find giving even more gratifying now that I have time to become more personally involved. America has been good to me, and I am grateful. I love my country, and I see my charitable work as a way to express appreciation. I've established the Lillian Vernon Foundation, which funds medical research, the arts, education, the homeless, and services for the elderly.

Wonderful friendships, including mine with Beverly Sills, are a terrific side benefit of those interests. Beverly is a remarkable, giving person—amusing, sharp, and compassionate. She knows how to call in her chips when one of her projects is in need. That's a trait I admire and am learning to apply.

There are moments when I wonder what my life would have been like had I taken a different road. In times of crisis

---

TAKE CARE OF YOURSELF

As you start your business, never forget that there are limits to the human body's endurance. If you find yourself working twelve hours a day, snatching food instead of sitting down to meals, and never taking time away from your company, you will hurt your business—but even more important, you will hurt yourself. You do a good job only if you are healthy and mentally alert. Time off is a good investment in your personal well-being and in the health of your business. Treat yourself to a lunch, a visit to the hairdresser, or an afternoon of shopping. Take a weekend off to have fun. You will return refreshed.

Exercises that you can do at home will help reduce tension and stress and keep you looking great. If you find that you make excuses to skip working out, you should consider joining a gym and going there on a regular schedule. A stress reduction seminar is perhaps a good investment. Face it, starting and running a business is very stressful and time-consuming. Anything you can do that helps you will enhance your ability to do a good job, to enjoy your achievements, and to move ahead more quickly.

---

and intense pressure, I sometimes think: I should have gone into antiques. I'd be presiding over an elegant shop on Madison Avenue—composed, tranquil, and surrounded by beautiful objects. What could be more serene and satisfying? But then I'll start to think about dust. Can you imagine how much time I'd be spending dusting those bow-back armchairs and ormolu plaques? No thank you. In the long run, my reality is far preferable to any of my fantasies.

Polishing and dusting notwithstanding, I do love antiques

and antique silver. I have collected pieces of my own, but among my most cherished possessions is a secretary that I inherited from my parents. They brought it to America from Leipzig. It is a fine Biedermeier secretary, which dates back to 1830, and its restrained, graceful lines adorn the dining room in my home. That's where I keep all my table linens. There is another piece of furniture that I've kept from my past. It's valuable to nobody but me, and it isn't graceful, either. The yellow Formica kitchen table at which I worked when I started my business in 1951, now occupies a place of honor at the entrance of our Virginia Beach facility.

The Test of Time

The Lillian Vernon Corporation will endure forever, whether I am here or not. I want to see it grow, and I want to contribute to that growth. I have found an experienced mail-order executive, Howard Goldberg, to take over the day-to-day management of the company. Laura Zambano has established a solid approach to merchandising, and Bob Mednick watches us all carefully. The company has all the mechanisms in place to stay young, flexible, and adventurous. Our staff is loyal and creative. They are people who love the company as passionately as I do. I have kept the company lean, without a top-heavy management stratum. That, in itself, is an accomplishment.

Not long ago, I started leafing through some of our old catalogs. Our best early products have stood the test of time. We still sell monogrammed belts, but they now sport a different look: they have solid brass buckles with three initials and are made of military webbing. Men's belts reverse from black to brown and have initialed brass buckles. The original bookmark, which sold for $1 in 1956, is, forty-one years later, still for sale. We've added a heart bookmark and an arrow bookmark that points to the line you are reading, but the basic concept remains what it was when Lillian Vernon began. Monogrammed luggage tags are another constant. We have changed the design from plain tags to Italian leather tags. But they remain useful and handsome—our original plan. Long before they became fashionable, we carried canvas luggage: suitcases, totes, carryalls. They, too, have been steady sellers throughout the years. I could list hundreds of sensible products that, although we may have redesigned them, still meet the same needs. The products in the Lillian Vernon catalogs are like children I've nurtured and watched grow up and change with the times.

And what about myself? Taking time off is something I wish I had done earlier in my life. I would still be where I am now even if there had been more vacations. There might have been less mayhem along the way, and people would not have accused me of being a workaholic, a term I really hate. No one seemed to understand that I have always found the problems of business fascinating. Solving them is for me a much greater and more satisfying challenge than filling in crossword puzzles. In the end, all the pieces have to fit.

How interested was I—I, and others have asked me—in making money just for the sake of money? My answer hasn't always been the same. When I began in 1951, I did it for money, hoping to increase our income by $50 a week. When I put $495 of our savings into that original ad in *Seventeen*, I figured that I might clear as much as two and a half cents for each dollar invested. In the end, I made $32,000. But making big bucks was never my main motivation, and I never had to drag myself to the office. The best answer to that question is that if I am going to go to work in order to make money, then I owe it to myself to make as much as I can. Still, money is round: it rolls, and it can roll away from you or toward you. That's why I always protected my name—my integrity—which is inextricably tied to my company and to me personally.

I know that I have power, but I want to use it wisely

because I also know that it affects the lives of many people: those I hire and those who buy from me. I would like to be thought of as a devoted mother, a good employer—a decent human being. People say that the business world makes you insensitive, that no powerful executive can be honest or upright. I strongly disagree. I have tried to deal honorably. I treasure my reputation and my good name, and I'm proud of the integrity my company has maintained over the years. Our profits are the report cards from our customers.

The Future

The mail-order business has to keep up with the technological times to stay afloat. Right now we are working on new ways to use the latest technology to improve our catalogs. We have joined with other catalog companies to produce a CD-ROM of our products. Customers will be able to browse through it, just as they can a paper catalog, and they can print out forms and place their orders. The number of consumers with CD-ROM–equipped computers continues to grow, and I see no signs of a slowdown. We have to change with everyone else and take advantage of new technology rather than be undone by it. I've been on QVC, the television shopping network, talked a little about the company, and demonstrated some of our products. It turned out to be an enjoyable venture.

Whatever plans may develop for the Lillian Vernon Corporation in the future, for the present I would like to travel for relaxation, adventure, and wonderful new items. I dream of spending a whole month in Paris. From my childhood days, Paris has always been my magic city, followed by London, Delhi, Amsterdam, Venice, and Milan, really anywhere in the world.

In so many ways, life is magic for me. Paolo has contributed to my happiness. Friends had doubts about our relationship. At first, I had doubts myself. But I've learned from experience to enjoy the good things in life rather than doubt and second-guess them into oblivion.

At a National Endowment for the Arts awards dinner held at the White House, I was invited to sit at the President's table. When the band began to play and people got up to dance, I hesitated. Given our age difference and that extraordinary guest list, I wasn't sure if it was proper for Paolo and me to join them. Eventually we did. At one point, I caught the First Lady's eye and saw her smile and nod. I knew then that my concerns had been unfounded. We were just another couple, dancing among so many others; not lost in the crowd, but a part of it.

At another dinner at the White House, I was shown to my overnight accommodations in the Lincoln bedroom. What rich and wonderful irony, I thought, that I should be here, a guest in this historic American room. I'd come to this country as an immigrant. My family had been seeking asylum and hoping to get by. Now I was a guest at the White House. Somehow I'd managed to take what are negatives—my shyness and insecurity—and used them to make something of my business and of my life. I saw then that the success of the Lillian Vernon Corporation had been the realization of my father's dreams and the validation of my own self-worth that I'd longed for. I had used the qualities at the core of my being to create the company.

Perhaps it wasn't the least bit ironic that I found myself in the Lincoln bedroom. Isn't opportunity what America is all about? Mine is truly an American story. This great country didn't make success easy, but it did handsomely reward all my hard work.

As I looked around at the understated, antique elegance of the Lincoln Room, and had a pleasant chat with the friendly ghost of Abraham Lincoln, imagine—from immigrant girl to the White House—only in America.

THE SUCCESSFUL ENTREPRENEUR'S TOOLKIT

From my years of experience as an entrepreneur in the mail-order business, I have formulated my own guidelines for successful ventures. And I'm pleased to pass my hard-earned insight on to others who are thinking of starting businesses of their own—mail order or not. All innovations originate with an idea—a vision. And every idea that led somewhere was supported by solid research and hard work. The successful entrepreneur learns to be a practical visionary. In the following pages, I share with you what I've learned about starting a business that thrives and endures.

Are You an Entrepreneur?

If you're thinking of starting your own business, here are ten questions you should ask yourself before you begin. Your answers should help you make your decision.

1: Do you have the necessary commitment? To succeed, you must feel passionate about the work you have chosen. Lukewarm enthusiasm will not sustain you through the challenges you will face in a start-up business.

2: Are you prepared to work extremely hard? Launching your own business demands long hours of labor. Are you sure you want to give up a good part of your social life: your weekends, golf games, and vacations? For your developing business to succeed, you will need to focus all your energies on it.

3: Are you sure you have the mental stamina and concentration to meet the demands your project will impose on you? If your attention flags, you may jeopardize your venture.

4: Do you accept new ideas easily? Do you treat other people's ideas with respect? Are you able to make decisions right away? An entrepreneur must be open-minded, flexible, and able to respond to new ideas.

5: How do you deal with problem solving? Are you prepared to spend time analyzing a problem and finding a solution? Or do you just close your eyes and hope for the best? No matter how carefully you plan, you are bound to run into an unforeseen problem now and then. Be prepared to cope with such a situation.

6: Are you ready to commit to the long term? A company's success is never an overnight miracle. That is one reason you must be absolutely certain that you love your work—there will be a lot of it.

7: What back-up resources do you have? Banks and other financial institutions seldom lend money to start-up businesses. Will family members or friends invest in your company or tide you over during a rough patch?

8: Are you good at concentrating on detail? Often, no one but you will be able to take care of small items. An entrepreneur's life is not one of ideas alone.

9: Are you ready to sit down and write a careful analysis of your business prospects? Without a best case/worst case scenario to guide you through the first years, you may be in for an unpleasant surprise or two. Be aware and be prepared.

10: Are you by nature an optimist? Mistakes and setbacks are bound to occur. Can you—without getting derailed or discouraged—learn from your mistakes?

Keep It Simple

Visionaries that they are, entrepreneurs easily fall so in love with their ideas that they inadvertently neglect the practical steps that will get their businesses going. Until you have some experience, it's wise to tame your ambitions. If you're going into mail order, limit your first product list to two or three items. By starting on a small scale, you will find it simpler to define your product and its potential market and, consequently, to budget your costs. Don't distract yourself with unnecessarily complicated goals.

Let's suppose, for example, that you have been making leather skirts and vests as presents for your family and friends. Over the years, you have accumulated all the necessary equipment for what has essentially been a hobby. After years of sewing these leather products, you have mastered the skills, and you think you can turn your hobby into a real moneymaker. Should you stick with skirts and vests or should you branch out into other leather goods, which you have never before attempted? My answer to you is: concentrate on what you know you can do.

Learn the Numbers

Learn to read balance sheets and income statements. You don't need an MBA from Harvard or Stanford. Local community colleges often offer accounting courses that are great for business beginners. You may think you can sidestep accounting ABCs by hiring an accountant you trust. Wrong.

Your accountant can calculate the figures, but you must interpret them so that you can respond quickly and appropriately. The numbers will tell you how a product is selling, but it will be up to you, as the owner of the business, to decide whether to increase production, change your advertising, or even drop that product.

The tasks that face a new entrepreneur range from the ridiculous to the sublime, but they cannot be ignored. Other business courses provide instruction on how to incorporate your company, fill out business tax forms, and comply with regulatory requirements. For instance, if you want to market cosmetics, you need to know that the cosmetics industry is heavily regulated by federal agencies. And as far as forming your company is concerned, you will need to decide whether to incorporate or register as a sole proprietorship in your own name. If you use a different name for your business bank account, you will file a DBA (Doing Business As) form with your county clerk. When you learn how to calculate expenses and income, you will have to be ready to lay out a realistic budget. Some entrepreneurs are really uncomfortable with the nitty-gritty of balance sheets and income statements. Their strengths lie in their inventiveness, and they have trouble focusing on outlays and income. But those whose businesses survive and prosper are the entrepreneurs who learn how to read such barometers of progress.

In addition to night-school courses, such business magazines as *Inc.*, *Income Opportunities*, and *Small Business Opportunities* are great sources of timely help to many entrepreneurs.

Research Your Market

Before you take any large steps, you should certainly examine the market for your product or service. Is there a need? Is the market near saturation? Assess your competition. Make sure you are offering something different from the rest. Is your product unique or sufficiently unusual to fill a neglected niche in the market?

Newspaper and magazine ads and mail-order catalogs can help you determine what's on the market. If you notice that the same ads for the same products appear consistently, you can be sure that there is a receptive market for them. Can you find room in that market alongside your competitors?

If there is a place for your merchandise, you should focus your investigation. If, for instance, you plan to sell to teenagers, then you need to research the demographics of the geographic area you wish to target. What is the average age of the population? Is it a high- or low-income area? SCORE—the initials stand for Service Corps of Retired Executives—is an organization whose members can probably give you good, solid advice. Its members are experienced businesspeople who can guide you to sources for the information you will need. SCORE's members aim to be mentors to entrepreneurs. Another good source of help may be your local bankers. It is their job to keep tabs on the local economy, and they can often help you figure out your best market.

Money! Money! Money!

A few people are lucky or smart enough to have money set aside for their new ventures. Others keep working at their salaried jobs until their new businesses can support them. There are still others, however, who can raise enough cash to support the start-up phases. You will need a realistic budget to show potential investors that you are a professional. When you are raising money, you are not only selling your business idea, you are also selling yourself. Banks and venture capitalists are not usually fertile sources of funds for new businesses or entrepreneurs with scant experience. A good track record is what makes the difference. As a beginner, your best bet is to persuade friends or family to help you out. You might approach the Small Business Administration about a loan guarantee, but that can develop into a long, drawn-out project. You might also find a partner with cash to invest, but entrepreneurs, as the originators of a business, often find it difficult to share decision making. So make absolutely sure that you can work together, and put everything in writing.

Be Prepared

If you're going to get into the mail-order business, it's best to start with an ad. That sounds easy, but in fact deciding where to place your ads will take considerable work. Here again, good research is called for. Invest in copies of a wide range of magazines that accept mail-order ads. Focus on those whose readership matches your target market. For example, if you aim to sell to young mothers, a chic fashion magazine won't be much help, nor will the *Wall Street Journal*. You can also place ads in your local newspaper, send out flyers, or post notices on a community bulletin board. Always remember that a 2 percent response is pretty much the best you can expect. Design your ad very carefully. Make sure that the headline is catchy, and that the copy sends the right message. If you are not trained in design, it may be worth hiring an experienced art director to produce your ad. After all, the ad is critical to your sales.

Be a Miser

Do not spend your hard-earned cash on anything but true necessities—stylish office furnishings and the like are peripheral to the ultimate success of your business. Good letterhead and business cards, however, are worth the investment: they link you to the outside world.

There are bound to be cash crunches, and if you aren't sufficiently established to borrow money, you may be forced to close. At first, take only the bare minimum out of the business. An expensive vacation or a new car may be tempting, but the needs of your fledgling company must come first. Remember, without a cash reserve you probably won't survive. Inadequate cash is the chief cause of business failure.

Know Your Customers

Your customers are the key to the survival of your business. Their responses will keep your company afloat. Therefore, woo them with all your creative energies.

In a world filled with so many products of average quality, a good entrepreneur understands the value of well-made products. Most people are willing to pay a little more for a product that endures.

Above and beyond every other consideration, be honest with your customers. The mail-order business once suffered badly from the dishonesty of some of its practitioners. Today, its reputation is good. Unless your customers trust you, they will certainly leave you. Your ads should never exaggerate. If your product is first-class, you certainly don't need to embellish it or try to mislead your customers.

Listen to your customers: they—better than most—can help you define your product. If people don't buy what you offer, you'd better recognize that you're on the wrong track. Response to a product is mail order's most reliable market research. If your product flops, redesign or drop it.

As your business grows, you will find it helpful to set up focus groups. They provide a direct approach to customer relations. Certain companies make a business of assembling focus-group meetings. You, the entrepreneur, sit, invisible, behind a one-way mirror through which you can observe— and videotape—the group's conversation. The group leader presents your product to the group and the participants react to it—for or against. Their comments may be revealing and should help to guide your merchandising.

Have the Courage to Take the Step

Moving from mail-order magazine and newspaper ads to publishing a catalog is the ambition of many entrepreneurs. It's a big step, which nobody should undertake without extensive market analysis, a substantial cash reserve, and a good staff. It will move your company to a different economic plane. The rewards will be bigger, but both work and responsibility will also expand. The cautionary message here is: be well prepared.

In the past, many small mail-order businesses started with a four- or six-page black-and-white catalog, but today almost all catalogs are in four colors and run to sixty pages and more. Obviously, they are expensive to produce, and the cost of postage is a significant factor.

You will need to expand your staff. As well as increasing the number of your employees, you will need an art director and, most likely, someone to write the catalog copy. If you have been the company merchandiser, you will probably need to hire an assistant. You will need help making sure that you have enough of the right products to fill the pages of a catalog.

At this stage, installation of an 800 number may make real sense. An 800 number simplifies the process of placing orders, and customers have grown to expect that convenience. Although it's an expensive service, the cost will pay for itself in increased orders. You must also be prepared to accept credit cards.

Plan on sending out at least four mailings a year. Depending on your line of products, you can expect certain times of the year to be more active than others. A gift catalog does best at Christmas. A sports catalog does well at

Christmas and also in the appropriate season. As long as you cover costs with a small margin of profit at other times of year, you can stay in business.

Search for Merchandise

Desirable merchandise is the foundation of all mail-order businesses. And nobody is more important to the success of a mail-order company than its merchandiser. Usually the founder of the business—the entrepreneur—takes charge of merchandising, which is nothing more or less than the hunt for the right products. This activity calls for a discerning eye, endurance, and the ability to make quick decisions. It entails buying trips to merchandising fairs, which take place all over the world. It calls for the strength, determination, and endurance to spend as many as nine hours a day walking through aisles crammed with vendors offering a vast, potentially overwhelming variety of products. You need to decide, then and there, what to buy—basing your decisions on rapid calculations of price, potential sales, and profit.

The best merchandiser is also a good diplomat. Bargaining for the best price is often the accepted practice—especially in Asia. But you must bargain with finesse. Alienating a manufacturer or a supplier is a short-sighted approach that you may regret sooner than you expect. In other countries, it's often advisable to hire an agent you can trust. Be prepared to hire and fire until you find somebody satisfactory. Never scrimp on the time, energy, and enthusiasm you devote to finding the best possible products for your catalog.

Remember, You Must Do It All

Here is where some entrepreneurs fail. They are filled with creative juices and total commitment to their business, but too often they don't understand that they must also be managers, administrators, even gofers—at least for a while. Some entrepreneurs do understand the art of management. As administrators they have to make sure that daily activities function smoothly. As gofers? Well, that includes everything from wrapping packages to making trips to the post office and brewing coffee. To run a fledgling mail-order company, the entrepreneur must curb his or her enthusiasm for expansion, learn to keep an analytical eye on the bottom line, and be prepared to undertake any job, no matter how menial. At the same time, entrepreneurs must never allow details to obstruct their overall vision for the business.

Growth Is a Two-Edged Sword

Suddenly your company takes off. You're enjoying a gratifying response to your catalogs; revenue is pouring in. Can you now sit back and simply let success happen? The answer is a firm no. Paradoxically, it's just at the moment of explosive growth that a mail-order company teeters on the brink of disaster. Rapid growth eats cash. You must hire staff to deal with the increase in business. You may have to make a significant investment in an up-to-date computer system. If fulfillment of orders lags because your system cannot handle the jump in customer orders, you really have no other choice.

This is the moment when a cash infusion is imperative. If your books show that you have run your company carefully, your cash flow can support interest payments, and you understand good business practices, your chances of getting a bank loan are good.

Focus, Focus, Focus

Peter Drucker, the father of modern management, has written that "concentration is the key to economic results."

That's advice every entrepreneur should heed. Is the business on track? Has it deviated from its original purpose? Concentrate on the products you know how to sell and on the market with which you are familiar. Stay in the business you know. Develop short-term and long-terms goals, but concentrate on present priorities.

By nature, entrepreneurs are optimists, but there is danger in a rosy, unrealistic assessment of a company's financial status and management. Self-confidence is a necessary character trait for someone starting a new business, but you must temper that enthusiasm with an ability to look at a situation with complete honesty and gritty objectivity. A strong streak of realism in the founding entrepreneur is key to success, especially in the early stages of business. Don't ignore flaws or mistakes, and never pretend that a false move wasn't important. Correct it. Self-deception can cover weakness only temporarily. Cold, dispassionate appraisals ward off future failures and lead instead to a flourishing business.

You can write to Lillian Vernon, or the Lillian Vernon Foundation, at 543 Main Street, New Rochelle, New York 10801.

To receive the Lillian Vernon Catalog, call 1-800-505-2250.

Visit us online at America Online, keyword Lillian Vernon, or www.lillianvernon.com